MAHATMA GANDHI
SELECTED POLITICAL WRITINGS

Mahatma Gandhi

Selected Political Writings

Edited, with Introduction, by
DENNIS DALTON

Hackett Publishing Company, Inc.
Indianapolis/Cambridge

Selections from the works of Gandhi are reprinted here by permission of
Navajivan Trust, Ahmedabad, India.

M. K. Gandhi: 1869–1948

Copyright © 1996 by Hackett Publishing Company, Inc.

Printed in the United States of America

00 99 98 97 96   1 2 3 4 5

For further information, please address
  Hackett Publishing Company, Inc.
  P. O. Box 44937
  Indianapolis, Indiana 46244-0937

Cover design by Listenberger & Associates
Text design by Dan Kirklin

Library of Congress Cataloging-in-Publication Data

Gandhi, Mahatma, 1869–1948.
    [Selections. 1996]
    Mahatma Gandhi: selected political writings/edited, with
  introduction, by Dennis Dalton.
        p. cm.
  Includes bibliographical references and index.
  ISBN 0-87220-331-X (hc.) ISBN 0-87220-330-1 (pbk.)
    1. Gandhi, Mahatma, 1869–1948—Philosophy. 2. Passive resistance.
  3. Liberty. I. Dalton, Dennis. II. Title.
  DS481.G3A25   1996
  954.03′5′092—dc20   95-47532
                                                                CIP

The paper used in this publication meets the minimum requirements of American
National Standard for Information Sciences—Permanence of Paper for Printed
Library Materials, ANSI Z39.48-1984.

∞

Contents

A Note on the Texts

The term "voluminous" seems an understatement when applied to Mahatma Gandhi's writings. His *Collected Works* [*CWMG*] constitute no fewer than one hundred volumes, each over four hundred pages of text; Gandhi wrote every word himself, as is evident especially in the intimacy of his autobiographical writing and in thousands of letters that reveal his mind with a frankness quite uncommon in public figures. It is significant that all of the criticisms of Gandhi's life draw on these texts: he kept no secrets.

Less "political" or "theoretical" than the writings of leaders like Lenin or Mao as they struggle with problems of Marxism, Gandhi's works are lucid and open. Yet his political thought is there, contained foremost in his core concepts of *satyagraha* and *swaraj*. These are not only key ideas to which he continually returns in these texts, but they are also central values that he keeps turning over and around as he evolves a philosophy of life. Because his *Collected Works* are arranged in chronological order, moving day by day through his newspaper articles and correspondence, speeches and party resolutions, pamphlets and books, one may trace closely the development of his thought. This short edition of his writings attempts to clarify his original contribution to political theory by setting forth as succinctly as possible his conceptions of power and freedom as they relate to other aspects of his philosophy.

The publication by the Indian government of Gandhi's *Collected Works* in both English and Hindi began in February 1956 and finished in October 1994 to mark Gandhi's 125th birthday. This huge effort was organized by the Publications Division of the Ministry of Information and Broadcasting, and it involved Navajivan Press, the original publisher of Gandhi's writings, and countless researchers who found and assembled materials on four continents. I am indebted for guidance and assistance to professors K. K. Swaminathan and C. N. Patel, editors of the *Works*, who discussed with me their handling and interpretations of the sources, and Pyarelal Nayar, Gandhi's personal secretary and biographer, who since 1965 has shared with me his own collection of Gandhi's writings before they later appeared in the *Works*.

Introduction

I could not help but think that had the protesters been more disciplined—
Gandhi-like—they could have achieved their objective of shutting it down.
—Robert S. McNamara

In likely and unlikely contexts, Mahatma Gandhi continues today to evoke
appreciation. A British historian, Eric Hobsbawm, recently observed that
this is because Gandhi "invented the politician as saint."[1] He is the rarest
of revolutionaries, representing disciplined and responsible political
action rather than what Robert McNamara deplored as he watched that
afternoon in 1967 from his Pentagon fortress: "an uncontrolled mob . . .
frightening but ineffective."[2] This was the antithesis of Gandhi, who as
he challenged authority remained civil, principled, restrained, and non-
violent in thought and deed. After all, he was called "Mahatma" or "Great
Soul" for a reason. How many other national leaders have maintained
power for three decades and consistently dignified politics?

During Gandhi's lifetime, political mass movements occurred around
the world in a wide variety of cultures, politicizing millions of people. India's struggle for freedom from British colonial rule was the longest and
largest of these movements. It began formally in 1885 with the creation of
the Indian National Congress and ended when India achieved independence in 1947. Gandhi assumed leadership of this movement in 1919 and
rapidly transformed it into a mass organization that mobilized India's
villages. The participation of a huge peasant population significantly included women at every level.

Other political giants like Hitler, Lenin, and Mao used their mass
movements to consolidate totalitarian regimes. Gandhi guided his nationalist movement to the establishment of India as the world's largest democracy, beginning a process of decolonization that would continue for
decades after his death. The most unique aspect of the Indian movement,
however, and the main reason for history's favorable judgment of Gandhi
is that it wielded power nonviolently. If not for this, then neither McNamara nor anyone else would see Gandhi, a rebel, as setting a standard for
correct political behavior.

Gandhi conceived his method of *satyagraha* (nonviolent power) in a culture that, stereotypes notwithstanding, is no less violent than American society. India today, as in Gandhi's era, is torn by religious extremism. No nation has a longer history of social conflict. An American journalist, A. M. Rosenthal, deploring the violence in India between Hindus and Muslims, observed that "Gandhi, founder of Indian freedom, used religion to combat bigotry, not promote it."[3] More precisely, he used nonviolence to combat the violence of both political extremism and religious fanaticism. He perceived early that India's real enemy was not merely imperialism but violence. To all those who promoted it—terrorists, communists, fascists—he replied, "I do not believe in short-violent-cuts to success. I am an uncompromising opponent of violent methods even to serve the noblest of causes. There is, therefore, really no meeting ground between the school of violence and myself."[4] Then he proceeded to demonstrate the superior power of nonviolence.

This century has witnessed to an unprecedented degree the terrible cost of political violence: violence perpetrated around the world by political systems, parties, or movements. Hundreds of millions of lives have been lost in war and revolution, in government repression and assassinations involving the widest range of ideologies or beliefs. Yet for all this agony we have not managed to establish an alternative method of conflict resolution that commands widespread allegiance among or within nations.

Gandhi's method of *satyagraha* offers an authentically new direction. Howard Gardner, in his study *Creating Minds*, groups Gandhi with Freud, Einstein, Picasso, and a few other twentieth-century thinkers or artists who were outstanding for their originality. He writes, "Gandhi was a thinker of the highest order. The conception of satyagraha was worked out as carefully as a philosophical system, with every step and its possible consequences carefully calibrated."[5] Because of Gandhi's renown as a political leader and reformer, his status as a political theorist may be missed. Yet the conceptual underpinnings of his political practice, provided by his theories of freedom and power, merit close analysis. The apex of his creative insight is his idea of nonviolence, among the most imaginative contributions to modern political theory.

At its present stage of development, nonviolent action in politics is no panacea; even Gandhi's strongest admirers recognize this. When Nobel Prize winners like Albert Einstein, Martin Luther King, Jr., Nelson Mandela, Aung San Suu Kyi, and the Dalai Lama all praise Gandhi as the political leader of our era most worthy of emulation,[6] it is not because they believe that nonviolence is an infallible remedy, a solution for every conflict in all circumstances. They realize that although *satyagraha* is in its infancy—a political technique in an early phase of experimentation—violence has proved politically dysfunctional. In terms of a cost-benefit analysis, it is priced far too high for what it delivers. Nelson Mandela wrote that he had determined from Gandhi's example "that violence threatens our aspirations for peace and reconciliation."[7] It is too costly for a new South Africa. This realization may not come easily, especially to one like Mandela who has suffered intolerable political persecution. Consider what the Dalai Lama or Aung San Suu Kyi have experienced of the scourges of political violence in Tibet and Burma. One might think that they would want retribution in kind. Instead, they seek nonviolent alternatives as inspired by Gandhi. Martin Luther King, Jr., expressed their sentiments when he said, "If humanity is to progress, Gandhi is inescapable. He lived, thought, and acted, inspired by the vision of humanity evolving toward a world of peace and harmony. We may ignore him at our own risk."[8]

Mohandas Karamchand Gandhi was born on October 2, 1869, into a Hindu family of moderate means in the town of Porbandar, on the west coast of India. He was the youngest of five children. His father, Kaba Gandhi, was an influential political figure, having served in several public positions. Gandhi describes him as "truthful, brave and generous, but short-tempered." His mother is portrayed as faultless: "deeply religious" to the point of "saintliness," yet with a "strong common sense." She impressed him most with her spirit of self-sacrifice. As a devout Hindu in pursuit of self-purification, "She would take the hardest vows and keep them without flinching. . . . To keep two or three consecutive fasts was nothing to her."[9] He makes clear that the decisive influence on his life came from his mother.

In his *Autobiography*, Gandhi portrays a childhood and adolescence far from ideal, describing himself as "very shy" and a "mediocre student" who felt betrayed by his closest friends. He recalls acute guilt feelings toward his father and intense jealousy of his child bride, Kasturbai, as they struggled through an arranged marriage beginning when they were both thirteen years old. Worst of all were his fears: "I was a coward. I used to be haunted by the fear of thieves, ghosts and serpents. I did not dare to stir out of doors at night. Darkness was a terror to me."[10] Courage and fearlessness became hard sought virtues.[11]

Lifelong lessons were learned from each of the adolescent "tragedies" that Gandhi reports in the early chapters of his autobiography. From an excruciating conflict with his father came redemption through a "clean confession," producing a sudden and unexpected "object-lesson in *Ahimsa* [nonviolence]": that "when such *Ahimsa* becomes all-embracing, it transforms everything it touches. There is no limit to its power."[12] From the horror of child marriage, which had first turned him into a "lustful" and possessive "jealous husband," he eventually learned to respect "woman as an incarnation of tolerance," to realize "that the wife is not the husband's bondslave, but his companion and his help-mate, and an equal partner in all his joys and sorrows—as free as the husband to choose her own path."[13] For a male living at this time in any society, this was an uncommon insight, yet consistent with Gandhi's later commitment as a political activist to the emancipation of women.[14]

At the end of the first part of his autobiography, Gandhi sums up the central values that he had formed by age eighteen, as he prepared to leave India for England. The syncretic spirit of Hinduism allowed him to define "religion . . . in its broadest sense, meaning thereby self-realization or knowledge of self."[15] This meant, on one hand, "that I had learnt to be tolerant of other religions," and, on the other, to be critical of dogmatic practices in Hinduism, particularly the institution of untouchability.[16] By his mid-teens, he had come to understand through his religion the relationship between truth and nonviolence. He concluded, first, that "truth is the substance of all morality. Truth became my sole objective. It began to grow in magnitude every day, and my definition of it also has been ever widening."[17] This understanding of truth as one's "sole objective" means that the supreme aim of human experience is knowledge of what Gandhi calls "the essential unity of man and for that matter of all that lives."[18]

The connection that he then made with nonviolent conduct was crucial for all that followed. If the highest truth is to perceive the unity of all being, then violence is impermissible because we are all part of one another, and thus to harm a person means inflicting injury on oneself. This realization came early in his education. He recalls a poem that he had learned in grammar school that concluded, "But the truly noble know all men as one/And return with gladness good for evil done." These "wonderful lines" "gripped my mind and heart" and "became such a passion with me that I began numerous experiments in it."[19] It is no wonder that a few years later, as a student in London reading the Bible, he would find and cherish "the Sermon on the Mount which went straight to my heart."[20]

Gandhi left India for London to study law in September 1888, one month before turning nineteen. At that time, he recalled, "It was an uncommon thing for a young man of Rajkot [his locality] to go to England." His family, however, had determined that a British law degree would advance their interests, and they pooled their resources to finance it. Gandhi's high-school curriculum, dictated and dominated by English masters there and abroad, had induced in him an awe of British civilization. Once the prospect of studying in London materialized, a sense of adventure overtook him; "my cowardice," he wrote, "vanished before the desire to go to England, which completely possessed me."[21] His mother required that he take three vows: "not to touch wine, woman and meat," solemn oaths, he said, to "keep me safe."[22]

Not so easily was he protected in London from an infatuation with everything English. Now began his extraordinary journey of mind and spirit, from being a colonized Indian in the British Empire to a leader of free India. This journey took him from an obsessive emulation of English values in his twenties and thirties to a radical rejection of Western civilization in his forties, and, finally, to a mature realization of what we identify today as his inclusive vision of humanity. Gandhi's value system, then, was not realized all at once: he struggled to develop it through constant reexamination, striving for a right fit between his evolving personal values and modes of political leadership.

He started at age nineteen in London by entering awkwardly into English society, determined to "be clumsy no more, but to try to become polished." Later he would call this "the all too impossible task of becoming an English gentleman," but at the time it had tragicomic aspects:

> The clothes after the Bombay cut that I was wearing were, I thought, unsuitable for English society and I got new ones. . . . I also went in for a chimney-pot hat costing nineteen shillings—an excessive price in those days. Not content with this, I wasted ten pounds on an evening suit made in Bond Street, the centre of fashionable life in London. I wasted ten minutes every day before a huge mirror, watching myself arranging my tie and parting my hair in the correct fashion. My hair was by no means soft, and every day it meant a regular struggle with the brush to keep it in position. Each time the hat was put on and off, the hand would automatically move towards the head to adjust the hair, not to mention the other civilized habit of the hand every now and then operating for the same purpose when sitting in polished society. As if all of this were not enough to make me look the thing, I directed my attention to other details that were supposed to go towards the making of an English gentleman. I was told it was necessary for me to take lessons in dancing, French and elocution.[23]

So it continued, a compulsion to ape the ways of his master.

Countless confessions have come from other such victims of colonialism or racism, describing the lethal process of trying to gain self-respect in a way that only brings self-alienation. The tale is told best by Malcolm X in his *Autobiography*. After pouring lye on his kinky hair to make it "real red—as straight as any white man's," he concludes,

> How ridiculous I was! Stupid enough to stand there simply lost in admiration of my hair now looking "white." . . . This was my first really big step toward self-degradation: when I endured all that pain, literally burning my flesh to have it look like a white man's hair. I had joined that multitude of Negro men and women in America who are brainwashed into believing that the black people are "inferior" and white people "superior" that they will even mutilate their God-created bodies to try to look "pretty" by white standards. . . . It makes you wonder if the Negro has completely lost his sense of identity, lost touch with himself.[24]

The typical pattern of behavioral change recorded in these stories is to abandon emulation for denunciation of the oppressor. Both Malcolm X and Gandhi follow this true to form. Malcolm's radical separatism as a Black Muslim is well known; Gandhi's separatist phase is not, because it seems so out of character with his mature attitude of inclusiveness. Yet just as Malcolm had to pass through the fire of black racism before he could realize the humanism of his final period, so Gandhi, too, pursued a tortuous path to liberation.

In 1893, London law degree in hand, Gandhi went to South Africa to pursue a legal career by representing members of the Indian community there, at a safe distance from the expectations and restrictions of his relatives in Rajkot.[25] No one then could have predicted that Gandhi would spend twenty-one years in South Africa, much less the extent to which that long experience would change his life.

The first big transformation came from his disillusionment with the British, whose empire then included South Africa. Gandhi had encountered racist abuse from the first days of his arrival in Durban; the epic film *Gandhi* dramatically portrays how he was assaulted because of his skin color. His emulative attitude, though, went very deep, and for years he excused such abuses as unrepresentative of the real spirit of British civilization, which he characterized as inherently just and fair. As late as 1905, after having practiced law in South Africa for twelve years, Gandhi could urge his Indian community: "We should not envy [Britain], but emulate its example."[26] By 1909, however, Gandhi, now at age forty, had changed drastically: "If India copies England, it is my firm conviction that she will be ruined."[27]

What explains this about-face? Gandhi's separatism began in the summer of 1906, with the British response to the "Zulu rebellion," an uprising that British soldiers suppressed with shocking brutality. Gandhi entered that summer so loyal to his colonial rulers that he volunteered to serve as a medic with the government against the Zulus. He soon discovered that what the British had characterized as a rebellion was really a massacre, often of innocent civilians. He at first consoled himself by attending to wounded Zulus, but soon his assumptions about English civilization, fixed for decades, completely collapsed.[28] Erik Erikson, in his psychobiography of Gandhi, incisively describes this moment: "the experience of witnessing the outrages perpetuated on black bodies by white he-men aroused in Gandhi both a deeper identification with the maltreated, and a stronger aversion against all male sadism—including such sexual sadism as he had probably felt from childhood to be part of all exploitation of women by men."[29] The connection that Gandhi apparently made with the oppression of women is significant: from this point on he sees racism, imperialism, and sexism as related, all distinct yet similar forms of domination.

Immediately after this experience, Gandhi's behavior signaled a return to some of the essential attitudes formed in childhood, particularly to his strong image of his mother taking vows of self-discipline. He accordingly imposed on himself a stricter code of moral restraint with a lifelong vow of celibacy (brahmacharya). This act liberated him: "I realized that a vow, far from closing the door to real freedom, opened it."[30] It freed him from family bonds to perform greater service for the community, enhancing his political potency[31] as he prepared to break with the colonial system through civil disobedience.[32]

The precise event that triggered the civil disobedience came only a month after the defeat of the Zulus. In August 1906 the British colonial government in Johannesburg gave notice of new legislation. All Indians were required to register with the police by giving fingerprints and noting other marks of identification. A substantial fine or three months in prison penalized those who failed to comply. Among Indians, the law quickly became known as the "Black Act." Gandhi, as a leader of his community, branded the new legislation discriminatory and humiliating because Indians were regarded as common criminals. He called a meeting of three thousand Transvaal Indians on September 11 in Johannesburg, and, at his initiative, they resolved to protest through mass civil disobedience. He made clear in moving the resolution that it was far different than any passed before: "It is a very grave resolution that we are making, as our existence in South Africa depends upon our fully observing it."[33] He insisted that it was so serious that it must be sealed by each person with an oath before God.

Much later Gandhi would refer to the events surrounding this meeting as the "advent of *satyagraha*," that is, the birth of his method of nonviolent action. The main ingredients were present here: a common perception of an extreme injustice and a conviction that civil disobedience could offer a remedy. This kind of direct action or "empowerment" meant, from the moment it was conceived, that a community's overcoming fear and recovery of self-respect could come through collective nonviolence.

His new method was initially described as "passive resistance," but within a year Gandhi rejected that term because it did not convey the active power of nonviolence. He then coined the term *satyagraha*, defined as the "force" of truth and love.[34] From the outset, therefore, Gandhi wanted to emphasize the special power of *satyagraha* by distinguishing it from passive resistance or what he called *duragraha*, "the force of bias." *Duragraha* is the counterfeit of *satyagraha* because it implies a wrong use of power, coming from a selfish obstinacy. The passive resister or *duragrahi* may avoid physical violence yet still harbor enmity and anger within, using nonviolence as a tactic but lacking commitment to its core values of understanding, openness, and respect for the adversary.[35]

Martin Luther King, Jr., understood this distinction when, following Gandhi, he rejected "passive resistance" as a misnomer. *Satyagraha*, King wrote,

> avoids not only external physical violence but also violence of spirit. The nonviolent resister not only refuses to shoot his opponent but he also refuses to hate him. . . . In the struggle for human dignity, the oppressed people of the world must not succumb to the temptation of becoming bitter or indulging in hate campaigns. . . . Along the way of life, someone must have sense enough and morality enough to cut off the chain of hate. This can be done by projecting the ethic of love to the center of our lives.[36]

Gandhi would most probably have applauded this interpretation, especially if he could have lived another ten years to see it actualized in the Montgomery bus boycott, the remarkable American *satyagraha* that started our civil-rights movement.

Gandhi's political theory at its most original contributes two ideas that are quintessentially his own: the first, for which he is renowned, his conception of the power of nonviolence or *satyagraha*; the second, integrally related, is his theory of freedom or *swaraj*. The Sanskrit word *swaraj* carried two distinct meanings in ancient India. It could denote, in a political sense, a sovereign kingdom's freedom from external control. It could also mean being liberated in an internal, spiritual, or psychological sense, as being free from illusion and ignorance, free to gain greater self-knowledge and consequent self-mastery. Obsessions with money and property or with ways of manipulating people were seen in this light as addictive forms of human bondage.

The *Bhagavad-Gita*, Hinduism's holiest book and Gandhi's primary text, viewed freedom as spiritual liberation. It described the free person as one who "acts without craving, possessiveness," and who "finds peace" in awareness of the "infinite spirit," thereby being "freed from delusion."[37] This is the key: to see beyond the illusion of separateness, to gain a vision of the unity of all being or the oneness of life. The prerequisite for this attainment is self-discipline. One must exercise control to focus on the essential nature of reality and distinguish it from transient illusions, from the myriad temptations and fleeting distractions that surround us. Thus the *Bhagavad-Gita* acclaimed the liberated sage as "the man of discipline" and affirmed, "Arming himself with discipline, seeing everything with an equal eye, he sees the self in all creatures and all creatures in the self."[38]

This is the philosophy of freedom that came from India's classical tradition to shape Gandhi's idea of *swaraj*. It defined freedom in a dual sense, having political and spiritual sides, but it gave most attention to the "internal" aspect of freedom, a higher consciousness attained through disciplined pursuit of self-awareness and knowledge. What mattered most to Gandhi was how *swaraj* could be connected to a whole nexus of other concepts, but especially to *satyagraha*, his idea of nonviolent power and truth.

These theories were initially developed in Gandhi's first major writing, *Hind Swaraj* (Indian Independence), published in 1909, three years after the civil disobedience movement in South Africa had begun. This short treatise consolidated his theories of freedom and power. Real *swaraj*, he proclaimed, demands "self-rule or self-control. The way to it is *satyagraha*: the power of truth and love."[39]

Several years after this extremely important book appeared, Gandhi reflected on his intention in writing it, explaining his original purpose in these terms:

It was written . . . in answer to the Indian school of violence, and its prototype in South Africa. I came in contact with every known Indian anarchist in London. Their bravery impressed me, but I feel that their zeal was misguided. I felt that violence was no remedy for India's ills, and that her civilization required the use of a different and higher weapon. . . . [*Hind Swaraj*] teaches the gospel of love in place of that of hate. It replaces violence with self-sacrifice. It pits soul-force [*satyagraha*] against brute-force.[40]

Six months before writing the book, Gandhi had spent three months in a Pretoria prison for civil disobedience. There he read Thoreau, and he was particularly impressed by this passage from *Civil Disobedience*: "I saw that, if there was a wall of stone between me and my townsmen, there was a still more difficult one to climb or break through before they could get to be as free as I was."[41] Gandhi liked this view of freedom and closely identified with Thoreau's imprisonment for civil disobedience sixty-three years earlier. He remarked on these lines from Thoreau that the individual who pursues truth through civil disobedience may be imprisoned, but "his soul is thus free," and "taking this view of jail life, he feels himself quite a free being." He concluded that a right understanding and enjoyment of freedom "solely rests with individuals and their mental attitude."[42]

There is no doubt that Thoreau's influence was considerable, second only to Tolstoy among non-Indian sources. Most elements of this influence are obvious: his prescription of civil disobedience, extending to tax resistance and imprisonment, to resist war and slavery. Less apparent, though, are the ways that Thoreau's ideas of truth and freedom appealed to Gandhi, that is, Thoreau's view of the enlightened individual on a "pilgrimage" to truth, and equally his concept of freedom as a state of mind or higher consciousness that required intense self-discipline.

Together with Thoreau, Gandhi revered Tolstoy, for his book *The Kingdom of God is Within You* revealed as none other "the infinite possibilities of universal love."[43] Tolstoy confirmed Gandhi's faith in nonviolence while Thoreau contributed to his ideas of freedom and power. These two brilliant visionaries, one American and the other Russian, so different from each other and from Gandhi, nevertheless affected the ideas in *Hind Swaraj* probably more than any of Gandhi's Indian contemporaries.

Hind Swaraj takes the form of a dialogue between "Reader" and "Editor." The former argues with haste and rashness terrorist ideas; the latter presents Gandhi's own case. At the outset, the Editor appears on the defensive. Then gradually he subdues the terrorist's storm. Ultimately the Reader yields to the force and novelty of an alternative that seems more revolutionary than his own method of violent insurrection. It is the Reader who initially poses the central question of the book, "What is *swaraj*?" Most of the text proceeds to set forth Gandhi's idea of freedom.

The Reader gives his version of *swaraj* first:

> As in Japan, so must India be. We must have our own navy, our own army, and we must have our own splendor, and then will India's voice ring through the world. . . . If the education we have received be any use, if the works of Spencer, Mill and others be of any importance, and if the English Parliament be the Mother of Parliaments, I certainly think that we should copy the English people.

The Editor disagrees:

> You have drawn the picture well. In effect it means this: that we want English rule without the Englishman. You want the tiger's nature, but not the tiger; that is to say, you would make India English. And when it becomes English, it will be called not Hindustan but Englishstan. This is not the *Swaraj* that I want. . . . It is as difficult for me to understand the true nature of *Swaraj* as it seems to you to be easy. I shall, therefore, for the time being, content myself with endeavoring to show that what you call *Swaraj* is not truly *Swaraj*.[44]

Gandhi believed that to achieve genuine freedom Indians must overcome their debilitating fear and awe of British rule, the source of their powerlessness. "Some Englishmen state that they took and they hold India by the sword," the Editor says. "Both these statements are wrong. The sword is entirely useless for holding India. We alone keep them."[45] The independence movement must attack the sources of this collaboration. First, then, "cultivate fearlessness. . . . *Satyagraha* cannot proceed a step without fearlessness. Those alone can follow the path of nonviolent resistance who are free from fear, whether as to their possessions, false honor, their relatives, the government, bodily injuries or death."[46] Such a psychological change is an absolute prerequisite for a free society.

The next step toward *swaraj* is to tackle long-overdue social reforms that have been hindered by the British presence. The first of these is the distrust and tension between Hindus and the large Muslim minority in India. Gandhi devotes most space to this problem and thus in a prophetic way foresees what will ultimately become the major obstacle to Indian independence. However much Gandhi will be accused later of misunderstanding the bases of Hindu-Muslim conflict, it cannot be said that he ignored it. From the beginning of his political career in South Africa, he gave this problem priority in his agenda of social reforms. In *Hind Swaraj* he contends that the allegation that there exists an "inborn enmity" and inevitable irreconcilability between Hindus and Muslims "has been

invented by our mutual enemy," the British, in order to divide and conquer. The remedy for this is to engender trust and tolerance among all
religions in India.[47]

The other reform that Gandhi advocates is essentially economic because it is directed at social elites, especially lawyers and physicians, but it
extends beyond them also to elitist institutions, from schools to means of
Western technology. He attacks modern systems of law, medicine, and
communication created by British imperialism, because Indians in these
professions were among the chief collaborators with colonialism. For taking this position Gandhi has earned scathing criticism for seemingly
wanting India to return to a preindustrial period. In fact, Gandhi was not
a reactionary but a democrat who desired social justice, economic equality,
and a secular state. He despaired of the arrogant indifference of Indian
elites to the masses; those elites wanted neither revolution nor social and
economic equality. *Hind Swaraj* marks the first salvo in a lifelong battle
against elitism by arguing that truly democratic use of machinery or medicine to improve the peasants' quality of life could come only if Indian
attitudes moved ahead to adopt egalitarian norms and fair distribution of
wealth.

The most original aspect of his reform program was an insistence that
everyone engage in manual labor, anathema for privileged classes given
their strong caste taboos. Gandhi's requirement in *Hind Swaraj* was that
lawyers and doctors must "take up a hand-loom" to spin homegrown cotton (*khadi*) and then even to wear it instead of British goods. This was
intended not only to spur boycott of English products but also to encourage identification with the masses, who could not afford imported cloth.
Gandhi's term for this form of resistance was *swadeshi*, meaning reliance
on the produce of one's own country.

The latter half of *Hind Swaraj* is devoted largely to establishing the relationship between freedom and power, of *swaraj* to *satyagraha*. "Real
swaraj is possible," he asserts, "only where *satyagraha* is the guiding force
of the people."[48] The term "force" is consistently used in defining *satyagraha*: "The force implied in this may be described as love-force, soul-
force. . . . The force of love is the same as the force of the soul or truth. We
have evidence of its working at every step. The universe would disappear
without the existence of that force." *Satyagraha* is contrasted with "brute-
force." Gandhi argues, "The force of arms is powerless when matched
against the force of love or the soul,"[49] a "force" found in the moral
universe comparable to the physical force of gravity. Nonviolent action

releases a natural power that when used correctly must have fundamental political, social, and economic consequences.

Hind Swaraj overflows with originality in its conceptualization of the connections between *swaraj* and *satyagraha*. Nowhere is this more evident than in Gandhi's creative interpretation of the logical relationship between the means and ends of action. The Editor tells his terrorist friend, "Your belief that there is no connection between the means and the end is a great mistake. . . . The means may be likened to a seed, the end to a tree; and there is just the same inviolable connection between the means and the end as there is between the seed and the tree. . . . We reap exactly as we sow."[50] Because the method is *satyagraha* and the end is *swaraj*, then true liberation comes only through the purest of means, the power of nonviolence.

Gandhi concludes his manifesto of freedom with an eloquence that would soon fire the Indian independence movement. Within a decade after finishing *Hind Swaraj* he would be leader of the Indian National Congress and thus of the freedom struggle. By that time these lines would be on the lips of thousands, literate or not:

> If we become free, India is free. And in this thought you have a definition of *Swaraj*. It is *Swaraj* when we learn to rule ourselves. It is, therefore, in the palm of our hands. Do not consider this *Swaraj* to be like a dream. There is no idea of sitting still. The *Swaraj* that I wish to picture is such that, after we have once realized it, we shall endeavour to the end of our life-time to persuade others to do likewise. But such *Swaraj* has to be experienced by each one for himself. One drowning man will never save another. Slaves ourselves, it would be a mere pretension to think of freeing others. . . . To blame the English is useless, they came because of us, and remain also for the same reason, and they will either go or change their nature only when we reform ourselves.[51]

No more emulation of the English. Gandhi had become by 1909 a full-fledged nationalist.

Gandhi returned to India in 1915. The long period in South Africa had provided an extended opportunity for successive *satyagrahas* or civil disobedience campaigns by the Indian minority there. These had climaxed in the "great march" of November 1913, which involved 2,221 men, women, and children in a mass protest against racist legislation. This had a dramatic impact, and before Gandhi left many of the grievances that Indians had suffered were effectively redressed. Unfortunately, after his departure the *apartheid* regime reasserted itself with renewed vigor; it is thus correct to say that "what Gandhi did to South Africa was less important than what South Africa did to him."[52] From his viewpoint in 1915, the experiment had proved successful; he was now eager to apply *satyagraha* to the larger context of India. And if ever there were a case for the importance of timing, when the historical moment is ripe for the ideal leader, then India after World War I presents a perfect example.

Although generals are rarely historians, sometimes historic struggles are best depicted by the combatants themselves, especially when they have a trained eye not only for details of combat but also for grand designs. Thucydides, the Athenian general and historian of ancient Greece, offers the best proof of this in his immortal analysis of the Peloponnesian War. The Indian independence movement found its Thucydides in Jawaharlal Nehru, one of the nonviolent generals in the nationalist struggle and afterward the first prime minister of independent India. Nehru was a fearless practitioner of civil disobedience as well as an astute analyst of the dynamics of Gandhi's power. Thucydides composed his history in exile; Nehru wrote his, *The Discovery of India*, as a political prisoner. As both historians reflected on the epic struggles that had immersed them, they recorded and interpreted decisive turning points that defined the destinies of their great civilizations. In his book, Nehru reveals the mood of India from 1914 to 1919, as well as the economic and psychological conditions that explain Gandhi's rise to power during this critical moment of its history.

Nehru's analysis focuses first on India at the beginning of World War I. He moves directly to the political scene, where the independence movement had reached a "low ebb chiefly because of the split in the [Indian National] Congress between the two sections, the so-called extremists and the moderates." This rampant factionalism produced a crisis, tearing the organization apart in 1907. The political in-fighting continued until 1919, when Gandhi unified the Congress under his leadership.

Nehru describes the economic conditions in detail. An enormous disparity of wealth had developed, with profits flowing "to the owners of foreign capital in Dundee and London" as well as "to swell the riches of Indian millionaires," whereas "the workers who had created these dividends lived at an incredibly low level of existence." Nehru provides graphic details of the appalling poverty that he witnessed, the severe deprivation of food, clothing, and shelter, through which "millions of men are starving and unemployed." The data are especially damning to the government because it cites official British reports, including one from a public-health director in Bengal that states that "the peasantry of that province were 'taking to a dietary on which even rats could not live for more than five weeks.'"

Then Nehru turns to the period immediately after the war. This was a critical moment in the history of British imperialism. The war had devastated the societies of winners and losers alike in Europe; Britain thus sought to rescue its domestic economy by increasing exploitation of its colonies. This inevitably worsened the political situation as government control became more authoritarian. Britain had a vast empire across the world, on which literally the sun never set, and India remained "the jewel in the crown" and thus the object of most imperial domination. The worst moments for Indians came in 1919 when, expecting some relief from the so-called victory of the Allies, they got repression instead. Nehru captures the mood:

> World War I ended at last, and the peace, instead of bringing us relief and progress, brought repressive legislation and martial law. A bitter sense of humiliation and a passionate anger filled our people. All the unending talk of constitutional reform and Indianization of the services was a mockery and an insult when the manhood of our country was being crushed and the inexorable and continuous process of exploitation was deepening our poverty and sapping our vitality. We had become a derelict nation.
>
> Yet what could we do to change this vicious process? We seemed to be helpless in the grip of some all-powerful monster; our limbs were paralyzed, our minds deadened. The peasantry were servile and fear-ridden; the industrial workers were no better. The middle classes, the intelligentsia, who might have been beacon-lights in the enveloping darkness, were themselves submerged in this all-pervading gloom. In some ways their condition was even more pitiful than that of the peasantry. Large numbers of them, *déclassé* intellectuals, cut off from the land and incapable of any kind of manual or technical work, joined the swelling army of the unemployed, and helpless, hopeless, sank ever deeper into the morass.[53]

The nadir of moral collapse in India for ruled and ruler alike came on April 13, 1919, with what became known in history as the Amritsar massacre. As Gandhi later wrote, this tragic instant of Indian history provided an indelible example of "to what lengths the British Government is capable of going, and what inhumanities and barbarities it is capable of perpetrating in order to maintain its power."[54] Thousands of Hindus and Sikhs had gathered in the town square of Amritsar, a city in the Punjab province of northern India for a religious holiday. Instead of a celebration they received a merciless fusillade from troops who fired relentlessly into the

crowd, for the British army commander, General Reginald Dyer, some-
how saw the gathering as a dangerous mob acting in defiance of his proclamation of martial law. Four hundred Indian civilians were killed and fif-
teen hundred wounded on that Sunday afternoon. In the hearings that
followed the tragedy, Dyer justified his action by testifying, "I think it was
a merciful thing. I thought that I should shoot well and shoot strong, so
that I or anybody else should not have to shoot again."[55]

Gandhi was repelled not only by Dyer's arrogance and the public ac-
claim he subsequently received in England, but also by the behavior of
Indians who cowered at the government's use of terror. He concluded
from the episode that imperialism in India had victimized colonizer and
colonized alike through its insidious climate of submission and domination. In an article on General Dyer, Gandhi wrote that obviously, "the loss
of innocent life [is] deplorable. But the slow torture, degradation and
emasculation that followed was much worse," as Indians were subsequently
subjected to unspeakable humiliations. In a "calculated, malicious" manner the British "tried to kill the soul of a nation."[56]

Nehru reflected in similar terms on the lessons of Amritsar: "Imperialism and the domination of one people over another is bad, and so is racialism. But imperialism plus racialism can only lead to horror and ultimately
to the degradation of all concerned with them."[57] In the midst of this
crisis of mutual dehumanization, Nehru posed the question, "What could
we do? How could we pull India out of this quagmire of poverty and de-
featism which sucked her in?" The way in which he frames his answer
presents a perceptive comment on Gandhi's sources of power:

And then Gandhi came. He was like a powerful current of fresh air that made
us stretch ourselves and take deep breaths; like a beam of light that pierced the
darkness and removed the scales from our eyes; like a whirlwind that upset
many things, but most of all the working of people's minds. He did not descend
from the top; he seemed to emerge from the millions of India, speaking their
language and incessantly drawing attention to them and their appalling condition. Get off the backs of these peasants and workers, he told us, all you who
live by their exploitation; get rid of the system that produces this poverty and
misery. Political freedom took new shape then and acquired a new content.
Much that he said we only partially accepted or sometimes did not accept at all.
But all this was secondary. The essence of his teaching was fearlessness and
truth, and action allied to these, always keeping the welfare of the masses in
view. The greatest gift for an individual or a nation, so we had been told in our
ancient books, was *abhaya* (fearlessness), not merely bodily courage but the absence of fear from the mind. Janaka and Yajnavalka had said, at the dawn of our

history, that it was the function of the leaders of a people to make them fearless. But the dominant impulse in India under British rule was that of fear—pervasive, oppressing, strangling fear; fear of the army, the police, the widespread secret service; fear of the official class; fear of laws meant to suppress and of prison; fear of the landlord's agent; fear of the moneylender; fear of unemployment and starvation, which were always on the threshold. It was against this all-pervading fear that Gandhi's quiet and determined voice was raised: Be not afraid. Was it so simple as all that? Not quite. And yet fear builds its phantoms which are more fearsome than reality itself, and reality, when calmly analyzed and its consequences willingly accepted, loses much of its terror.

So, suddenly, as it were, that black pall of fear was lifted from the people's shoulders, not wholly of course, but to an amazing degree. As fear is close companion to falsehood, so truth follows fearlessness. The Indian people did not become much more truthful than they were, nor did they change their essential nature overnight; nevertheless a sea-change was visible as the need for falsehood and furtive behaviour lessened. It was a psychological change, almost as if some expert in psycho-analytical methods had probed deep into the patient's past, found out the origins of his complexes, exposed them to his view, and thus rid him of that burden.

There was that psychological reaction also; a feeling of shame at our long submission to an alien rule that had degraded and humiliated us, and a desire to submit no longer whatever the consequences might be.[58]

The power of Gandhi's new style of leadership was restorative, therapeutically designed to recover India's spirit and identity. The twenty-eight-year national movement that followed the Amritsar massacre mobilized the country in three successive civil-disobedience campaigns. These occurred ten years apart: the first nonviolent noncooperation campaign (1919–22), the mass civil disobedience movement or "salt *satyagraha*" (1930–31), and the wartime resistance or "Quit India" movement against the government (1942–44). Each of these targeted specific issues, such as the salt tax in 1930, but all had the general aim of attaining *swaraj*.

The first noncooperation campaign stunned not only the British Raj but also the whole world because of its efficacy and novelty. Nothing of this nature in politics had been seen before. Mass strikes had been tried in various European contexts, but the ideology and practice of *satyagraha*, with its creedal affirmation of nonviolence, was entirely new. The campaign was filled with surprises, culminating in Gandhi's decision to end it when Indians engaged in an episode of violence, as Gandhi describes in "The Crime of Chauri Chaura," included in this volume. His decision was challenged by other leaders who could not accept that one violent incident should end the campaign. Gandhi insisted that his purpose was not merely to dislodge the British but to prepare his people for *swaraj*, a kind of freedom that could not be defined merely as "independence." He explained, "independence may mean license to do as you like. *Swaraj* is positive. Independence is negative. . . . *Swaraj* may, therefore, be rendered as disciplined rule from within."[59] This call for restraint was an improbable attitude for a revolutionary leader. In his history of the twentieth century, aptly entitled *The Age of Extremes*, Eric Hobsbawm analyzes the first noncooperation campaign's extraordinary success. The government, he observes, admitted its "great anxiety" when India so quickly became "ungovernable," and at this critical moment, Gandhi chose to impose discipline, persuading the Congress not "to plunge their country into the savage darkness of an uncontrollable insurrection by the masses. . . . After Gandhi called off the campaign of civil disobedience early in 1922, on the grounds that it had led to the massacre of policemen in one village, it can reasonably be claimed that British rule in India depended on his moderation—far more than on police and army."[60] Such "moderation" came only as a product of scrupulous training in disciplined nonviolent action.

The second civil-disobedience movement a decade later acted on the premise that the country was more prepared for mass action. Although the campaign produced substantial violence from the government, none came from the civil resisters or, as they were called, *satyagrahis*. This campaign was the "salt *satyagraha*" because Gandhi had chosen to offer resistance to the salt tax. Civil disobedience commenced with what became known in history as the "salt march." Gandhi and eighty of his followers walked over two hundred miles in twenty-four days to the Indian seacoast, where they defied the government's monopoly on salt production by manufacturing their own from natural salt deposits on the shores. Hundreds of thousands followed Gandhi's example and were arrested for breaking the salt laws. Everyone understood from the outset that the real point of the campaign was not simply to manufacture salt but to produce disciplined civil disobedience.

Yet, even after these campaigns of nonviolence, India in the end did plunge into mass violence with the civil war that surrounded its attaining independence in August 1947. Gandhi, now in his late seventies, threw his whole being into reversing the tide of religious violence that consumed northern India. In November and December 1946, following the initial outbreak of Hindu-Muslim conflict in Bengal, Gandhi, incredibly, walked 116 miles through forty-seven villages in affected areas, stopping for brief periods in the worst of them. By January 1947 he had succeeded in

Bengal. He then rushed to Bihar, another scene of religious or "communal" conflict, in this case wholesale killing of Muslims by Hindus. His valiant efforts to restore peace persisted throughout the next year until his assassination.

By far the most dramatically effective *satyagrahas* at this time were his fasts to protect Muslims in Calcutta and Delhi. Indeed, the sheer power of his two major fasts of September 1947 and January 1948 now had an impact on Indians comparable to that of his salt march on the British. They demonstrated as never before the remarkable range of his technique of *satyagraha*. Nicholas Mansergh, in a close historical analysis of this period, concluded that "in this last year of his life, Gandhi's influence was transcendent. . . . It was his preaching of his doctrine of nonviolence more than any other single factor that stood between India and bloodshed on a frightful scale."[61] Another British historian, E. W. R. Lumby, was fascinated with Gandhi's Calcutta fast because it seemed almost magically to transform that city. Lumby, not given to overstatement, nevertheless believed that in Calcutta Gandhi "had in fact worked a miracle, perhaps the greatest of modern times."[62] If British historians of this quality are any measure, then history's judgment of Gandhi is clear: his leadership demonstrated for over forty years of political action the undeniable power of nonviolence.

In Delhi and Calcutta, Gandhi would announce his intentions at his regular prayer meetings. These daily meetings attracted thousands of Muslims and Hindus to hear him begin with readings from their sacred texts and then appeal to their common faith in God, to the urgent need for trust and tolerance. Extremist elements in both religious communities, often themselves traumatized by family casualties in the civil war, despised Gandhi for his insistence on forgiveness. They wanted revenge.

On January 30, 1948, as Mohandas Gandhi entered the prayer grounds in Delhi, Nathuram Godse kneeled before him, then rose to fire three bullets in Gandhi's chest. Gandhi died instantly. Godse was captured, tried, and executed. At his trial, he explained his motives. A well-educated, orthodox Brahman, thirty-five-year-old editor of a Hindu weekly in Maharashtra, he had planned the murder carefully· "I sat brooding intensely on the atrocities perpetrated on Hinduism and its dark and deadly future if left to face Islam outside and Gandhi inside." He believed that war against Muslims must accelerate.[63] But his assassination of Gandhi had the opposite effect of what he had intended. The Hindu community was stunned with guilt and remorse that the Mahatma had been murdered by one of their own. They determined to end the conflict, and the killing stopped.

If Gandhi's assassination had resulted in an increase of killing and re-
crimination, then it might be deemed a judgment on the futility of non-
violence. As it happened, in the eloquent words of a prominent Muslim
politician in India of that time, "Gandhi's assassination had a cathartic effect and throughout India men realized with a shock the depth to which
hatred and discord had dragged them. The Indian nation turned back
from the brink of the abyss and millions blessed the memory of the man
who had made redemption possible."[64] There was no higher tribute to his
life than the impact of his death, his final statement for *swaraj*.

NOTES

1. Eric Hobsbawm, *The Age of Extremes: A History of the World, 1914–1991*
(New York: Pantheon, 1994), 208. Another appreciative comment from an American political leader is found in Al Gore's *Earth in the Balance* (New York: Penguin,
1993), 14.

2. Robert S. McNamara, *In Retrospect: The Tragedy and Lessons of Vietnam*
(New York: Random House, 1995), 305.

3. A. M. Rosenthal, "Hindus Against Hindus," *New York Times*, March 5,
1993, A29.

4. Mohandas Karamchand Gandhi, *The Collected Works of Mahatma Gandhi*
(hereafter *CWMG*) (Delhi: Publications Division, Ministry of Information and
Broadcasting, Government of India, 1961) 25: 424.

5. Howard Gardner, *Creating Minds: An Anatomy of Creativity Seen Through
the Lives of Freud, Einstein, Picasso, Stravinsky, Eliot, Graham, and Gandhi* (New
York: Basic Books, 1993), 355.

6. Albert Einstein wrote that "in our age of moral decay [Gandhi] was the
only statesman who represented that higher conception of human relations in the
political sphere to which we must aspire with all our powers." (*Einstein on Peace*,
edited by Otto Nathan and Heinz Norden [New York: Avenel Books, 1981], 468.)
Martin Luther King's judgment is cited in note 8. Nelson Mandela said, "I could
never reach the standard of morality, simplicity and love for the poor set by the
Mahatma. . . . Gandhi was a human without weaknesses." (*New York Times*, January 30, 1995, A6.) Aung San Suu Kyi, winner of the Nobel Peace Prize in 1991 for
her nonviolent resistance to government tyranny in Burma (Myanmar), "acquired
her lasting admiration for the principles of non-violence embodied in the life and
philosophy of Mahatma Gandhi." (Suu Kyi, *Freedom From Fear* [New York: Penguin, 1991], 291.) His Holiness, The Dalai Lama of Tibet, relates the inspiration
of Gandhi: "I had and still have unshaken faith in the doctrince of nonviolence
which he preached and practiced. Now I made up my mind more firmly to follow
his lead whatever difficulties might confront me. I determined more strongly than
ever that I could never associate myself with acts of violence." (*My Land and My
People* [New York: McGraw-Hill, 1962], 146.)

7. Nelson Mandela, "Gandhi the Prisoner: A Comparison," *Indian Horizon* vol. 43, no. 4 (1994): 17.

8. Martin Luther King, Jr., *The Words of Martin Luther King, Jr.* (New York: New Market Press, 1983), 71.

9. *CWMG* 39: 7–9.

10. Ibid., 21.

11. Susanne and Lloyd Rudolph have incisively analyzed how Gandhi's sense of cowardice drove him to formulate a "new courage" for himself and for India in their admirable study *Gandhi* (Chicago: University of Chicago Press, 1983), 6–38.

12. *CWMG* 39: 28.

13. Ibid., 25.

14. See the superb analysis of this subject by Madhu Kishwar, "Gandhi on Women," *Economic and Political Weekly* vol. 20, no. 40 (October 5, 1985), and no. 41 (October 12, 1985).

15. *CWMG* 39: 31.

16. Gandhi relates in his *Autobiography* that early in his South African experience, "Hindu defects were pressingly visible to me. If untouchability could be a part of Hinduism, it could but be a rotten part or an excrescence." His total opposition to untouchability was evident then and never ceased to be a central issue in his program of social reforms. *CWMG* 39: 113.

17. Ibid., 33–34.

18. *CWMG* 25: 390.

19. *CWMG* 39: 34.

20. Ibid., 61.

21. Ibid., 36.

22. Ibid., 37–38.

23. Ibid., 46–47.

24. Malcolm X, *The Autobiography of Malcolm X* (New York: Ballantine, 1973), 54.

25. Stephen Hay thoroughly examines Gandhi's thinking at this time in "Gandhi's Reasons for Leaving Rajkot for South Africa in 1893," a paper presented to the 1995 Meeting of the Association for Asian Studies, Washington, D.C., April 9, 1995.

26. *CWMG* 5: 117.

27. *CWMG* 10: 18.

28. In one of the chapters in his *Autobiography* on the Zulu rebellion ("Heart Searchings") Gandhi relates how this event, unlike his earlier experience in the Boer War (1899–1902), "brought home to me the horrors of war." *CWMG* 39: 252.

29. Erik Erikson, *Gandhi's Truth* (New York: W. W. Norton, 1969), 194.

30. *CWMG* 39: 167.

31. The phrase "self-control and political potency" is used by Susanne and Lloyd Rudolph in *Gandhi*, 38–62, as the focal point of their analysis of Gandhi's change of behavior.

32. *CWMG* 39: 168. This chapter in his *Autobiography* is entitled "Brahmacharya." He expresses the connections between his personal and political conduct when relating the critical turn of events in the summer of 1906: "In about a month of my returning [to Johannesburg], the foundation of Satyagraha was laid. As though unknown to me, the brahmacharya vow had been preparing me for it. Satyagraha had not been a preconceived plan. It came on spontaneously."

33. *CWMG* 5: 419–20.

34. *CWMG* 16: 368–69; and 29: 254–55.

35. *CWMG* 14: 63–65.

36. Martin Luther King, Jr., *Stride Toward Freedom* (New York: Harper and Row, 1958), 103–4.

37. *The Bhagavad-Gita* 2: 71–72, translated by Barbara Stoler Miller (New York: Bantam, 1986), 39.

38. Ibid., 6: 29, 66; and 8: 30, 119.

39. *CWMG* 10: 64. Although Gandhi usually translated *satyagraha* as the "force" of truth or of love, power seems a preferable translation because force is often associated with violence.

40. *CWMG* 19: 277.

41. "Essay on Civil Disobedience," in *Walden and Other Writings*, edited by J. W. Krutch (New York: Bantam, 1989), 97.

42. *CWMG* 10: 65, 189. A year later after completing *Hind Swaraj*, Gandhi singled out Thoreau as among those whom he had "endeavoured humbly to follow" in writing the book, and he lists *Civil Disobedience* and *Life Without Principle* among those works that had influenced him most.

43. *CWMG* 39: 131.

44. *CWMG* 10: 16.

45. *CWMG* 10: 23.

46. Ibid., 53.

47. Ibid., 29.

48. Ibid., 51.

49. Ibid., 46–47.

50. Ibid., 43.

51. Ibid., 63.

52. B. R. Nanda, *Mahatma Gandhi* (Bombay: Allied Publishers, 1958), 121.

53. Jawaharlal Nehru, *The Discovery of India* (Bombay: Asia Publishing House, 1967), 377–78.

54. *CWMG* 29: 380.

55. Quoted in Robert Payne, *The Life and Death of Mahatma Gandhi* (London: The Bodley Head, 1969), 340.

56. *CWMG* 18: 45–46.

57. Nehru, *Discovery of India*, 344.

58. Ibid., 379–80.

59. *CWMG* 45: 263–64.

60. Hobsbawm, *The Age of Extremes*, 211.

61. Nicholas Mansergh, *The Commonwealth and the Nations* (London: Royal Institute of International Affairs, 1958), 142.

62. E. W. R. Lumby, *The Transfer of Power in India, 1945–1947* (London: Allen and Unwin, 1954), 193.

63. Quoted in *The Essential Gandhi*, edited by Louis Fischer (New York: Vintage Books, 1962), 368.

64. Humayun Kabir, "Muslim Politics, 1942–47," in *The Partition of India*, edited by C. H. Philips and M. D. Wainwright (London: Allen and Unwin, 1970), 405.

Part I
SATYAGRAHA:
THE POWER
OF NONVIOLENCE

INTRODUCTION

This selection from Gandhi's writings is organized around his two integrally related ideas of satyagraha *(power of nonviolence) and* swaraj *(freedom). The first part of these readings comprises Gandhi's thinking about nonviolent power, its strengths and limitations, and how it can flow forcefully from attitudes of truth and love. In the second part, on freedom, Gandhi argues that nonviolence liberates us from cycles of destructive behavior by connecting personal and political freedoms.*

"Power is of two kinds," Gandhi believed. "One is obtained by the fear of punishment and the other by acts of love. Power based on love is a thousand times more effective. . . ."[1] Nonviolence is not only ethically superior to violence, it also can be stronger; but it is often diluted or contaminated by anger or enmity and its power undermined. Gandhi tried to explain the problem of using nonviolent power in these terms: "The word satyagraha *is often most loosely used and is made to cover veiled violence. But as the author of the word I may be allowed to say that it excludes every form of violence, direct or indirect, and whether in thought, word or deed. It is a breach of* satyagraha *to wish ill to an opponent or to say a harsh word to him or of him with the intention of doing harm. And often the evil thought or the evil word may, in terms of* satyagraha, *be more dangerous than actual violence used in the heat of the moment.* Satyagraha *is gentle, it never wounds. It must not be the result of anger or malice. It was conceived as a complete substitute for violence."[2]*

The first entry is from Gandhi's column in Young India, *a weekly newspaper that he edited throughout his long public career. He often answered questions in this paper, chosen from the thousands that he received from around the world. His responses in this article show his concern for using nonviolent power in a spirit of truth. The concluding sentences also reveal his refusal to generalize about Germans in 1927, trusting in them as in the British, an attitude that had mixed results yet remained characteristic of his approach.*

TRUTH IS ONE

A Polish Professor writes:

I am reading with intense joy your fascinating articles in Young India and wish to impress upon you the truth that they are the source of power not only for your own country but for the world. And as you have such a wide spiritual experience, may I ask you one question to be answered if possible in Young India? It is a very important fundamental question to which an answer from you would have a great value. Do you admit that there is in human thought some absolute certainty, as for instance as to God and prayer, where we might be said to have reached perfect unchangeable truth? Now my fundamental question is, on what particular points do you change your opinion? And what guarantee can these changes leave as to the unshaken truth of what remains certain? How can we distinguish opportunistic change of opinion from the permanence of an absolute certainty in essentials? Can you define in what things we may change and what kind of things remain unchangeable? Is independence of each country or people one of those absolute truths, or is there some innate incapacity in some nations for self-government and in others an innate for governing such incapable nations, as the Germans profess to have a capacity for governing other nations and thus justify their ruling ambition?

[Gandhi replied:] Without in any shape or form endorsing the claim to the powers that the writer ascribes to me, I would in all humility endeavour to answer his questions. My own conscious claim is very simple and emphatic. I am a humble but very earnest seeker after truth. And in my search, I take all fellow-seekers in uttermost confidence so that I may know my mistakes and correct them. I confess that I have often erred in my estimates and judgments. As for instance, whereas I thought from insufficient data that the people of Kheda were ready for civil disobedience, I suddenly discovered that I had committed a Himalayan miscalculation, and saw that they could not offer civil disobedience inasmuch as they had not known what it was to tender willing obedience to laws which might be even considered irksome but not immoral. Immediately I made the discovery, I retraced my steps. A similar error of judgment was committed by me what I presented what had been described as the Bardoli ultimatum.*

---

*The references to Kheda and Bardoli, districts in India where Gandhi believed civil disobedience was used prematurely in 1919 and 1922, are discussed in *CWMG* 39: 373–75 and 22: 302–5. These are two significant examples of his determination to call off resistance campaigns when he deemed discipline and training inadequate.

I had then believed that the country, that is the people, had been awakened and touched by the movement, had understood the utility of nonviolence. I discovered my error within twenty-four hours of the delivery of the ultimatum and retraced my steps. And inasmuch as in every case I retraced my steps, no permanent harm was done. On the contrary, the fundamental truth of non-violence has been made infinitely more manifest that it ever has been, and the country has in no way been permanently injured. . . .

I claim to have no infallible guidance or inspiration. So far as my experience goes, the claim to infallibility on the part of a human being would be untenable, seeing that inspiration too can come only to one who is free from the action of pairs of opposites, and it will be difficult to judge on a given occasion whether the claim to freedom from pairs of opposites is justified. The claim to infallibility would thus always be a most dangerous claim to make. This however does not leave us without any guidance whatsoever. The sum total of the experience of the sages of the world is available to us and would be for all time to come. Moreover, there are not many fundamental truths, but there is only one fundamental truth which is Truth itself, otherwise known as Non-violence. Finite human being shall never know in its fullness Truth and Love which is in itself infinite. But we do know enough for our guidance. We shall err, and sometimes grievously, in our application. But man is a self-governing being, and self-government necessarily includes the power as much to commit errors as to set them right as often as they are made. . . .

I do think that independence of each country is a truth in the same sense and to the same extent that independence of each man is. There is, therefore, no inherent incapacity for self-government in any country or nation and therefore no inherent capacity for governing other nations. No doubt my correspondent honestly thinks that Germans profess to have a God-given capacity for ruling over other nations. But if there are German imperialists, there are also humble German democrats, who are content if they can quietly govern themselves.[3]

In early 1922, the British government in India was reeling from the effects of Gandhi's national campaign of nonviolent noncooperation. Yet at this moment of the movement's extraordinary success, there occurred an outbreak of violence. On February 5, in a village of northern India named Chauri Chaura, what began as a nonviolent demonstration suddenly turned ugly. The local police who had provoked the demonstrators were overwhelmed and murdered. Gandhi was horrified. In the following article, he explains why he felt compelled to call off the campaign until "by strict discipline and purification we regain the moral confidence required."

THE CRIME OF CHAURI CHAURA

God spoke clearly through Chauri Chaura. I understand that the constables who were so brutally hacked to death had given much provocation. They had even gone back upon the word just given by the Inspector that they would not be molested, but when the procession had passed the stragglers were interfered with and abused by the constables. The former cried out for help. The mob returned. The constables opened fire. The little ammunition they had was exhausted and they retired to the Thana [police station] for safety. The mob, my informant tells me, therefore set fire to the Thana. The self-imprisoned constables had to come out for dear life and as they did so, they were hacked to pieces and the mangled remains were thrown into the raging flames.

It is claimed that no non-co-operation volunteer had a hand in the brutality and that the mob had not only the immediate provocation but they had also general knowledge of the high-handed tyranny of the police in that district. No provocation can possibly justify the brutal murder of men who had been rendered defenseless and who had virtually thrown themselves on the mercy of the mob. And when India claims to be non-violent and hopes to mount the throne of Liberty through non-violent means, mob-violence even in answer to grave provocation is a bad augury. . . . Non-violent attainment of self-government presupposes a non-violent control over the violent elements in the country. Non-violent non-co-operators can only succeed when they have succeeded in attaining control over the hooligans of India, in other words, when the latter also have learnt patriotically or religiously to refrain from their violent activities at least whilst the campaign of non-co-operation is going on. The tragedy at Chauri Chaura, therefore, roused me thoroughly.

The drastic reversal of practically the whole of the aggressive program may be politically unsound and unwise, but there is no doubt that it is religiously sound, and I venture to assure the doubters that the country will have gained by my humiliation and confession of error.

The only virtue I want to claim is Truth and Non-violence. I lay no claim to superhuman powers. I want none. I wear the same corruptible flesh that the weakest of my fellow beings wears and am therefore as liable to err as any. My services have many limitations, but God has up to now blessed them in spite of the imperfections.

For, confession of error is like a broom that sweeps away dirt and leaves the surface cleaner than before, I feel stronger for my confession. And the cause must prosper for the retracing. Never has man reached his destination by persistence in deviation from the straight path. . . .

The tragedy of Chauri Chaura is really the index finger. It shows the way India may easily go if drastic precautions be not taken. If we are not to evolve violence out of non-violence, it is quite clear that we must hastily retrace our steps and re-establish an atmosphere of peace, re-arrange our program and not think of starting mass civil disobedience until we are sure of peace being retained in spite of mass civil disobedience being started and in spite of Government provocation.

. . . Some of us err in spite of ourselves. But some others among us sin willfully. They join Volunteer Corps well knowing that they are not and do not intend to remain non-violent. We are thus untruthful even as we hold the Government to be untruthful. We dare not enter the kingdom of Liberty with mere lip homage to Truth and Non-violence.

Suspension of mass civil disobedience and subsidence of excitement are necessary for further progress, indeed indispensable to prevent further retrogression. I hope, therefore, that by suspension every Congressman or woman will not only not feel disappointed but he or she will feel relieved of the burden of unreality and of national sin.

Let the opponent glory in our humiliation or so-called defeat. It is better to be charged with cowardice and weakness than to be guilty of denial of our oath and sin against God. It is a million times better to appear untrue before the world than to be untrue to ourselves.

And so, for me the suspension of mass civil disobedience and other minor activities that were calculated to keep up excitement is not enough penance for my having been the instrument, however involuntary, of the brutal violence by the people at Chauri Chaura.

I must undergo personal cleansing. I must become a fitter instrument able to register the slightest variation in the moral atmosphere about me. My prayers must have much deeper truth and humility about them than they evidence. And for me there is nothing so helpful and cleansing as a fast accompanied by the necessary mental co-operation.

I know that the mental attitude is everything. Just as a prayer may be merely a mechanical intonation as of a bird, so may a fast be a mere mechanical torture of the flesh. Such mechanical contrivances are valueless for the purpose intended. Again, just as a mechanical chant may result in the modulation of voice, a mechanical fast may result in purifying the body. Neither will touch the soul within.

But a fast undertaken for fuller self-expression, for attainment of the spirit's supremacy over the flesh, is a most powerful factor in one's evolution. After deep consideration, therefore, I am imposing on myself a five days' continuous fast, permitting myself water. It commenced on Sunday evening; it ends on Friday evening. This is the least I must do.

. . . I am in the unhappy position of a surgeon proved skill-less to deal with an admittedly dangerous case. I must either abdicate or acquire greater skill. . . .

All fasting and all penance must as far as possible be secret. But my fasting is both a penance and a punishment, and a punishment has to be public. It is penance for me and punishment for those whom I try to serve, for whom I love to live and would equally love to die. They have unintentionally sinned against the laws of the Congress though they were sympathizers if not actually connected with it. Probably they hacked the constables—their countrymen and fellow beings—with my name on their lips. The only way love punishes is by suffering. I cannot even wish them to be arrested. But I would let them know that I would suffer for their breach of the Congress creed. I would advise those who feel guilty and repentant to hand themselves voluntarily to the Government for punishment and make a clean confession. I hope that the workers in the Gorakhpur district will leave no stone unturned to find out the evil-doers and urge them to deliver themselves into custody. But whether the murderers accept my advice or not, I would like them to know that they have seriously interfered with swaraj operations, that in being the cause of the postponement of the movement in Bardoli, they have injured the very cause they probably intended to serve. I would like them to know, too, that this movement is not a cloak or a preparation for violence. I would at any rate suffer every humiliation, every torture, absolute ostracism and death itself to prevent the movement from becoming violent or a precursor of violence. I make my penance public also because I am now denying myself the opportunity of sharing their lot with the prisoners. The immediate issue has again shifted. We can no longer press for the withdrawal of notifications or discharge of prisoners. They and we must suffer for the crime of Chauri Chaura. The incident proves, whether we wish it or not, the unity of life. . . . By strict discipline and purification we regain the moral confidence required. . . .

If we learn the full lesson of the tragedy, we can turn the curse into a blessing. By becoming truthful and non-violent, both in spirit and deed . . . we can establish full swaraj.[4]

"Satyagraha is like a banyan tree with innumerable branches," Gandhi wrote. "Civil disobedience is one such branch, satya *(truth) and* ahimsa *(non-violence) together make the parent trunk."⁵ The quotation from the* Bhagavad-Gita *in the Introduction, which says that the sage "sees the self in all creatures and all creatures in the self," suggests the connectedness of all being that for Gandhi links* satya *with* ahimsa*. Because of our spiritual unity, to hurt another is to violate oneself. As Gandhi observes in the next article, the word* satya *is derived from* sat, *meaning "to be," so the highest truth is to know the ground of our being and he is "but striving to serve that truth."*

WHAT IS TRUTH?

There is a story in the gospel, in which a judge inquired, "What is truth?", but got no answer. . . .

The fact remains, that the question posed by that judge has not been answered. . . .

Beyond limited truths there is one absolute Truth which is total and all-embracing. But it is indescribable, because it is God. Or say, rather, God is Truth. . . . Other things, therefore can be true only in a relative sense.

He . . . who understands truth, follows nothing but truth in thought, speech and action, comes to know God and gains the secr's vision of the past, the present and the future. He attains *moksha* [liberation] though still encased in the physical frame.

If we get one single person, before the 31st of December, who would practice truth to such perfection, swaraj should be ours this very day.

Some of us are no more than *satya-agrahis*, those, in other words, who aspire to follow truth scrupulously, but they hardly succeed in doing so even in the limited sphere of speech. We thus see that observance of the vow of truth is no easy matter.

. . . I never claim anything beyond a sincere endeavour to keep the vow of truth. It never happens that I tell a lie deliberately. I do not remember having deliberately told a lie any time in my life, except on one occasion when I cheated my revered father. It has become part of my nature to speak the truth and act in accordance with truth. But it is impossible for me to claim that truth, which I perceive but dimly, has become part of my life. I am not beyond indulgence in unconscious exaggeration or self-praise or taking interest in describing my achievements. There is a shade of un-truth in all these and they will not stand the test of truth. A life wholly filled with the spirit of truth should be clear and pure as crystal. Untruth cannot survive even for a moment in the presence of such a person. No one can deceive a man who always follows truth, for it ought to be impossible that untruth will not be exposed in his presence. The most difficult vow to keep is the vow of truth. Out of lakhs* who may strive to follow truth, only a rare person will succeed completely in the course of his present life. . . .

The word *satya* [truth] comes from *sat*, which means "to be," "to exist." Only God is ever the same through all time. A thousand times honor to him who has succeeded, through love and devotion for this satya, in opening out his heart permanently to its presence. I have been but striving to serve that truth. I have, I believe, the courage to jump from the top of the Himalayas for its sake. At the same time, I know that I am still very far from that truth. As I advance towards it, I perceive my weakness ever more clearly and the knowledge makes me humble. It is possible to be puffed up with pride so long as one does not know one's own insignificance. But once a man sees it, his pride melts away. Mine melted away long ago. . . .

The sun's light does not need to be pointed out. Truth shines with its own light and is its own proof. In these evil times, it is difficult to follow truth in such perfection but I know it is not impossible. If a large number from among us strive to follow it even in some measure, we can win swaraj. We can also win it if a few of us pursue it with utmost consciousness. Only, we must be sincere. It will not do merely to make a show of following truth. It does not matter if we follow truth only to the extent of one anna in a rupee,† but it must be truth and not something else. The little measure of it which we follow must not, in any circumstances, be mixed with deliberate falsehood. It is my earnest desire that, in this holy yajna [sacrifice], all of us will learn to follow truth as a matter of principle.[6]

. . . I am but a seeker after Truth. I claim to have found the way to it. I claim to be making a ceaseless effort to find it. But I admit that I have not yet found it. To find Truth completely is to realize oneself and one's destiny, i.e., to become perfect. I am painfully conscious of my imperfections, and therein lies all the strength I possess, because it is a rare thing for a man to know his own limitations.

If I was a perfect man, I own I should not feel the miseries of my neighbors as I do. As a perfect man I should take note of them, prescribe a remedy and compel adoption by the force of unchallengeable Truth in me.

*One lakh = 100,000.
†One rupee = sixteen annas.

But as yet I only see as through a glass darkly and therefore have to carry convictions by slow and laborious processes, and then too not always with success.[7]

The Congress aims at reaching *purna* [complete] swaraj through Truth and Non-violence. And it will fail in so far as the *kisans* [peasants] fail to observe these two cardinal principles. You are millions. When millions become untruthful and violent, it will mean self-destruction. You will therefore suffer injury without retaliation.[8]

. . . Whether I retain my hold on the youth of Bengal or any other province or I do not, I must proclaim my creed from the house-top. Freedom of India's starving millions is attainable only through Truth and Ahimsa.[9]

Gandhi's theory and practice of nonviolence is primarily a product of Hinduism, but Christianity reinforced it in vital respects. He relates in his Autobiography *how the New Testament, "especially the Sermon on the Mount went straight to my heart. I compared it with the* Gita," *and "my young mind tried to unify the teaching" of these two religious texts.[10] He found in both the central value of nonviolence. Among modern thinkers, he was drawn especially to Leo Tolstoy, whose influence proved unique because of his Christian anarchism, which emphasized nonviolence as an essential mode of everyday conduct. "Tolstoy's* The Kingdom of God Is Within You," *he says in the* Autobiography, *"overwhelmed me. It left an abiding impression on me."[11]*

Tolstoy died in 1910. He first corresponded with Indian nationalists in 1908, and later directly with Gandhi, who had sent him a copy of Hind Swaraj. *The article that follows accompanied Gandhi's translation, from English to Gujarati, of Tolstoy's initial "Letter to a Hindoo" (dated December 14, 1908), which Gandhi had found so inspirational. This response was written at the same time that Gandhi composed* Hind Swaraj, *and the bibliography to that book confirms Tolstoy's substantial influence by citing five of his works, far more than any other author. When Gandhi answered him in August 1910, he mentioned that he had named his settlement in South Africa* Tolstoy Farm.[12]

PREFACE TO LEO TOLSTOY'S "LETTER TO A HINDOO"

Count Tolstoy is a Russian nobleman. He has had his full share of life's pleasures, and was once a valiant soldier. He has no equal among European writers. After much experience and study, he has come to the conclusion that the political policies generally followed in the world are quite wrong. The chief reason for that, according to him, is that we are vengeful, a habit unworthy of us and contrary to the tenets of all religions. He believes that to return injury for injury does harm both to ourselves and our enemy. According to him, we should not retaliate against anyone who may injure us, but reward him with love instead. He is uncompromising in his loyalty to the principle of returning good for evil.

He does not mean by this that those who suffer must seek no redress. He believes rather that we invite suffering on ourselves through our own fault. An oppressor's efforts will be in vain if we refuse to submit to his tyranny. Generally, no one will kick me for the mere fun of it. There must be some deeper reason for his doing so. He will kick me to bend me to his will if I have been opposing him. If, in spite of the kicks, I refuse to carry out his orders, he will stop kicking me. It would make no difference to me whether he did so or not. What matters to me is the fact that his order is unjust. Slavery consists in submitting to an unjust order, not in suffering ourselves to be kicked. Real courage and humanity consist in not returning a kick for a kick. This is the core of Tolstoy's teaching. . . .

To me Tolstoy's letter is of great value. Anyone who has enjoyed the experience of the Transvaal struggle will perceive its value readily enough. A handful of Indian satyagrahis have pitted love or soul-force against the might of the Transvaal Government's guns. That is the central principle of the Tolstoy's teaching, of the teaching of all religions. *Khuda-Ishwar* [God] has endowed our soul with such strength that sheer brute force is of no avail against it. We have been employing that strength against the Transvaal Government not out of hatred or with a view to revenge, but merely in order to resist its unjust order.

But those who have not known what a happy experience satyagraha can be, who have been caught up in the toils of this huge sham of modern civilization, like moths flitting round a flame, will find no interest in Tolstoy's letter all at once. Such men should pause for a moment and reflect.

Tolstoy gives a simple answer to those Indians who appear impatient to drive the whites out of India. We are [according to Tolstoy] our own slaves, not of the British. This should be engraved in our minds. The whites cannot remain if we do not want them. If the idea is to drive them out with firearms, let every Indian consider what precious little profit Europe has found in these.

Everyone would be happy to see India free. But there are as many views as men on how that can be brought about. Tolstoy points out a simple way to such men.

Tolstoy has addressed his letter to a Hindu and that is why it cites
thoughts from Hindu scriptures. Such thoughts, however, are to be found
in the scriptures of every religion. They are such as will be acceptable to
all, Hindus, Muslims and Parsis. Religious practices and dogmas may differ, but the principles of ethics must be the same in all religions. I therefore advise all readers to think [only] of ethics. . . .

It is a mere statement of fact to say that every Indian, whether he own
up to it or not, has national aspirations [for independence]. But there are
as many opinions as there are Indian nationalists, as to the exact meaning
of that aspiration and more especially as to the methods to be used to attain the end.

One of the accepted and "time-honored" methods to attain the end is
that of violence. The assassination of Sir Curzon Wylie* was an illustration in its worst and [most] detestable form of that method. Tolstoy's life
has been devoted to replacing the method of violence for removing tyranny
or securing reform by the method of non-resistance to evil. He would
meet hatred expressed in violence by love expressed in self-suffering. He
admits of no exception to whittle down this great and divine law of Love.
He applies it to all the problems that worry mankind.

When a man like Tolstoy, one of the clearest thinkers in the western
world, one of the greatest writers, one who, as a soldier, has known what
violence is and what it can do, condemns Japan for having blindly followed
the law of modern science, falsely so-called, and fears for that country
"the greatest calamities," it is for us to pause and consider whether, in our
impatience of English rule, we do not want to replace one evil by another
and a worse. India, which is the nursery of the great faiths of the world,
will cease to be nationalist India, whatever else it may become, when it
goes through the process of civilization in the shape of reproduction on
that sacred soil of gun factories and hateful industrialism, which has reduced the people of Europe to a state of slavery and all but stifled among
them the best instincts, which are the heritage of the human family.

If we do not want the English in India, we must pay the price. Tolstoy
indicates it.

Do not resist evil, but also yourselves participate not in evil, in the violent
deeds of the administration of the law courts, the collection of taxes and, what
is more important, of the soldiers, and no one in the world will enslave you,

*Political aide-de-camp to the Secretary of State for India, shot dead in London
by a Punjabi student, Madan Lal Dhingra, on July 1, 1909.

passionately declares the sage of Yasnaya Polyana. Who can question the truth of what he says?[13]

Gandhi's originality as a thinker and political leader appears most dramatically in his theory and practice of nonviolence. No one before in history had conceived of nonviolence and applied it to politics like him. Although Gandhi was inspired by the Hindu concept of ahimsa *(literally, non-injury), as well as by Christianity and the writings of Tolstoy and Thoreau, none of these influences provided a blueprint for him to follow when he developed his conception of* satyagraha. *The following articles contain the basic elements in his idea of nonviolence as he formulated it in the first decade after he returned to India from South Africa. Conceptual connections between nonviolence and truth,* swaraj *and* satyagraha, *as well as a defense of nonviolent resistance as a courageous method capable of succeeding where violence must fail, appeared first in* Hind Swaraj. *Here they are sharpened as he applies them to the freedom struggle in India. The ancient idea of* ahimsa *assumes unprecedented forms.*

ON AHIMSA

Though my views on ahimsa are a result of my study of most of the faiths of the world, they are now no longer dependent upon the authority of these works. They are a part of my life and if I suddenly discovered that the religious books read by me bore a different interpretation from the one I had learnt to give them, I should still hold the view of ahimsa as I am about to set forth here.

Our shastras seem to teach that a man who really practices ahimsa in its fullness has the world at his feet, he so affects his surroundings that even the snakes and other venomous reptiles do him no harm. This is said to have been the experience of St. Francis of Assisi.

In its negative form, it means not injuring any living being, whether by body or mind. I may not therefore hurt the person of any wrong-doer, or bear any ill will to him and so cause him mental suffering. . . .

In its positive form, ahimsa means the largest love, the greatest charity. If I am a follower of ahimsa, I must love my enemy. I must apply the same rule to the wrong-doer who is my enemy or a stranger to me, as I would to my wrong-doing father or son. This active *Ahimsa* necessarily includes truth and fearlessness. . . . A man cannot then practice ahimsa and be a coward at the same time. The practice of ahimsa calls forth the greatest courage.[14]

NON-VIOLENCE

When a person claims to be non-violent, he is expected not to be angry with one who has injured him. He will not wish him harm; he will wish him well; he will not swear at him; he will not cause him any physical hurt. He will put up with all the injury to which he is subjected by the wrongdoer. Thus non-violence is complete innocence. Complete non-violence is complete absence of ill will against all that lives. It therefore embraces even sub-human life not excluding noxious insects or beasts. They have not been created to feed our destructive propensities. If we only knew the mind of the Creator, we should find their proper place in His creation. Non-violence is therefore, in its active form, goodwill towards all life. It is pure Love. I read it in the Hindu scriptures, in the Bible, in the Koran.

Non-violence is a perfect state. It is a goal towards which all mankind moves naturally though unconsciously. Man does not become divine when he personifies innocence in himself. Only then does he become truly man. In our present state, we are partly men and partly beasts and, in our ignorance and even arrogance, say that we truly fulfill the purpose of our species when we deliver blow for blow and develop the measure of anger required for the purpose. We pretend to believe that retaliation is the law of our being, whereas in every scripture we find that retaliation is nowhere obligatory but only permissible. It is restraint that is obligatory. Retaliation is indulgence requiring elaborate regulating. Restraint is the law of our being. For, highest perfection is unattainable without highest restraint. Suffering is thus the badge of the human tribe.

The goal ever recedes from us. The greater the progress, the greater the recognition of our unworthiness. Satisfaction lies in the effort, not in the attainment. Full effort is full victory.

Therefore, though I realize more than ever how far I am from that goal, for me the Law of complete Love is the law of my being. Each time I fail, my effort shall be all the more determined for my failure. . . .

A drop of water must yield to the analyst the same results as a lakeful. The nature of my non-violence towards my brother cannot be different from that of my non-violence to the universe, it must still satisfy the same test . . .

The political non-violence of the non-co-operator [in the civil disobedience campaign of 1920–22] does not stand this test in the vast majority of cases. Hence the prolongation of the struggle. Let no one blame the unbending English nature. The hardest "fibre" must melt in the fire of love.

I cannot be dislodged from the position because I know it. When British or other nature does not respond, the fire is not strong enough, if it is there at all. Our non-violence need not be of the strong, but it *has* to be of the truthful. We must not intend harm to the English or to our co-operating countrymen if and whilst we claim to be non-violent. But the majority of us *have* intended harm, and we have refrained from doing it because of our weakness or under the ignorant belief that mere refraining from physical hurt amounted to due fulfillment of our pledge. Our pledge of non-violence excludes the possibility of future retaliation. Some of us seem, unfortunately, to have merely postponed the date of revenge.

Let me not be misunderstood. I do not say that the policy of non-violence excludes the possibility of revenge when the policy is abandoned. But it does most emphatically exclude the possibility of future revenge after a successful termination of the struggle. Therefore, whilst we are pursuing the policy of non-violence, we are bound to be actively friendly to English administrators and their co-operators. . . .

Swaraj by non-violent means can therefore never mean an interval of chaos and anarchy. Swaraj by non-violence must be a progressively peaceful revolution such that the transference of power from a close corporation to the people's representatives will be as natural as the dropping of a fully ripe fruit from a well-nurtured tree. I say again that such a thing may be quite impossible of attainment. But I know that nothing less is the implication of non-violence. And if the present workers do not believe in the probability of achieving such comparatively non-violent atmosphere, they should drop the non-violent program and frame another which is wholly different in character. If we approach our program with the mental reservation that, after all, we shall wrest the power from the British by force of arms, then we are untrue to our profession of non-violence. If we believe in our program, we are bound to believe that the British people are not unamenable to the force of affection as they are undoubtedly amenable to force of arms. For the unbelievers, the [alternative is] . . . a rapid but bloody revolution probably never witnessed before in the world. I have no desire to take part in such a revolution. I will not be a willing instrument for promoting it.[15]

MY PATH

I am conscious of the fact that the truth for which I stand has not yet been fully accepted by India. It has not yet been fully vindicated. My work in India is still in the experimental stage.

My path is clear. Any attempt to use me for violent purposes is bound to fail. I have no secret methods. I know no diplomacy save that of truth. I have no weapon but non-violence. I may be unconsciously led astray for a while but not for all time. I have therefore well-defined limitations, within which alone I may be used. . . .

I am yet ignorant of what exactly Bolshevism is. I have not been able to study it. I do not know whether it is for the good of Russia in the long run. But I do know that in so far as it is based on violence and denial of God, it repels me. I do not believe in short-violent-cuts to success. Those Bolshevik friends who are bestowing their attention on me should realize that however much I may sympathize with and admire worthy motives, I am an uncompromising opponent of violent methods even to serve the noblest of causes. There is, therefore, really no meeting ground between the school of violence and myself. But my creed of non-violence not only does not preclude me but compels me even to associate with anarchists and all those who believe in violence. But that association is always with the sole object of weaning them from what appears to me to be their error. For experience convinces me that permanent good can never be the outcome of untruth and violence.[16]

"ON THE VERGE OF IT"

I am your follower and have gone to jail under your leadership and guidance. . . . I now feel very much shaken in my faith in your reasoning and politics. I am not a revolutionary but I am on the verge of being a revolutionary. If you answer these questions satisfactorily, you may save me. . . .

What is more inhuman and terrible, rather what is more violent, to let 33 millions suffer, stagnate and perish, or a few thousand be killed [in a violent revolution]? What would you prefer, to see the slow death of a mass of 33 millions through sheer degeneration, or killing of a few hundred of people? If it is proved that by killing a few hundred, we can put a stop to the degeneration of 33 millions, will you object to violence on principle?

[Gandhi replied:] There is no principle worth the name if it is not wholly good. I swear by non-violence because I know that it alone conduces to the highest good of mankind, not merely in the next world but in this also. I object to violence because, when it appears to do good, the good is only temporary; the evil it does is permanent. I do not believe that the killing of even every Englishman can do the slightest good to India. The millions will be just as badly off as they are today, if someone made it possible to kill off every Englishman tomorrow. The responsibility is more ours than that of the English for the present state of things. The English will be powerless to do evil if we will but do good. Hence my incessant emphasis on reform from within.

But, before the revolutionary, I have urged non-violence not on the highest ground of morality but on the lower ground of expedience. I contend that the revolutionary method cannot succeed in India. If an open warfare were a possibility, I may concede that we may tread the path of violence that the other countries have and at least evolve the qualities that bravery on the battlefield brings forth. But an attainment of swaraj through warfare I hold to be an impossibility for any time that we can foresee. Warfare may give us another rule for the English rule but not self-rule [swaraj] in terms of the masses. The pilgrimage to swaraj is a painful climb. It requires attention to details. It means vast organizing ability, it means penetration into the villages solely for the service of the villagers. In other words it means national education, i.e., education of the masses. It means an awakening of national consciousness among the masses. It will not spring like the magician's mango. It will grow almost unperceived like the banyan tree. A bloody revolution will never perform the trick. Haste here is most certainly waste. . . .

Tyrants are, indeed, obdurate. The English tyrant is obduracy personified. But he is a multi-headed monster. He refuses to be killed. He cannot be paid in his own coin, for he has left none for us to pay him with. I have a coin that is not cast in his mint and he cannot steal it. It is superior to any he has yet produced. It is non-violence. . . .

Let my friend understand the implications of non-violence. It is a process of conversion. I am convinced. I must be pardoned for saying it that my out-and-out non-violence has converted many more Englishmen than any amount of threats or deeds of violence. I know that when conscious non-violence becomes general in India swaraj will not be far.[17]

LETTER TO NARANDAS GANDHI

July 28/31, 1930

The path of Truth is as narrow as it is straight. Even so is that of ahimsa. It is like balancing oneself on the edge of a sword. By concentration an acrobat can walk on a rope. But the concentration required to tread the path of Truth and ahimsa is far greater. The slightest inattention brings one tumbling to the ground. One can realize Truth and ahimsa only by ceaseless striving. . . .

Thus step by step we learn how to make friends with all the world; we realize the greatness of God, of Truth. Our peace of mind increases in spite of suffering; we become braver and more enterprising; we understand more clearly the difference between what is everlasting and what is not; we learn how to distinguish between what is our duty and what is not. Our pride melts away and we become humble. Our worldly attachments diminish and likewise the evil within us diminishes from day to day. . . . Not to hurt any living thing is no doubt a part of ahimsa. But it is its least expression. The principle of ahimsa is hurt by every evil thought, by undue haste, by lying, by hatred, by wishing ill of anybody. . . .

. . . Without ahimsa it is not possible to seek and find Truth. Ahimsa and Truth are so intertwined that it is practically impossible to disentangle and separate them. They are like the two sides of a coin, or rather of a smooth unstamped metallic disc. Who can say which is the obverse and which is the reverse? Nevertheless, ahimsa is the means and Truth is the end. Means to be means must always be within our reach, and so ahimsa becomes our supreme duty and Truth becomes God for us. If we take care of the means, we are bound to reach the end sooner or later. If we resolve to do this, we shall have won the battle. Whatever difficulties we encounter, whatever apparent reverses we sustain, we should not lose faith but should ever repeat one *mantra*: "Truth exists, it alone exists. It is the only god and there is but one way of realizing it; there is but one means and that is ahimsa. I will never give it up. May the God that is Truth, in whose name I have taken this pledge, give me the strength to keep it."[18]

LOVE NOT HATE

A telegram from Allahabad says Pandit Motilal Nehru, Pandit Jawaharlal Nehru, Pandit Shamlal Nehru and Mr. George Joseph, Editor of the *Independent*, have been arrested [for civil disobedience, as prominent leaders in the independence movement]. It was received at 11 o'clock last night. It positively filled me with joy. I thanked God for it. . . .

But my joy, which I hope thousands share with me, is conditional upon perfect peace being observed whilst our leaders are one after another taken away from us. *Victory is complete if non-violence reigns supreme in spite of the arrests. Disastrous defeat is a certainty if we cannot control all the elements so as to ensure peace.* We are out to be killed without killing. We have stipulated to go to prison without feeling angry or injured. We must not quarrel with the condition of our own creating.

On the contrary our non-violence teaches us to love our enemies. By non-violent non-co-operation we seek to conquer the wrath of the English administrators and their supporters. We must love them and pray to God that they might have wisdom to see what appears to us to be their errors. It must be the prayer of the strong and not of the weak. In our strength must we humble ourselves before our Maker.

In the moment of our trial and our triumph let me declare my faith, I believe in loving my enemies. I believe in non-violence as the only remedy open to the Hindus, Mussulmans [Muslims], Sikhs, Parsis, Christians and Jews of India. I believe in the power of suffering to melt the stoniest heart. The brunt of the battle must fall on the first three. The last named three are afraid of the combination of the first three. We must by our honest conduct demonstrate to them that they are our kinsmen. We must by our conduct demonstrate to every Englishman that he is as safe in the remotest corner of India as he professes to feel behind the machine gun.

Islam, Hinduism, Sikhism, Christianity, Zoroastrianism and Judaism—in fact religion is on its trial. Either we believe in God and His righteousness or we do not. My association with the noblest of Mussulmans has taught me to see that Islam has spread not by the power of the sword but by the prayerful love of an unbroken line of its saints and fakirs. . . .

What must we then do? Surely remain non-violent and yet strong enough to offer as many willing victims as the Government may require for imprisonment. Our work must continue with clock-work regularity. Each province must elect its own succession of leaders. . . .

We must hold the Congress at any cost in spite of the arrest of everyone of the leaders unless the Government dissolve it by force. And if we are neither cowed down nor provoked to violence but are able to continue national work, we have certainly attained swaraj. For no power on earth can stop the onward march of a peaceful, determined and godly people.[19]

As Robert McNamara has suggested, the behavior of the civil resister matters: the more civil, the more effective. Gandhi emphasized the qualities of civil conduct in all respects, meaning that the satyagrahi *must consistently show restraint, discipline, in the words of the article that follows, "good manners and humility." Intemperate and rude behavior revealed a lack of personal control, anger or "violence of the spirit," just as an absence of humility showed an arrogance of mind, a dogmatic outlook. Gandhi felt that he could not trust such attitudes under fire, and he usually required that those who accompanied him, as on the salt march, affirm that they believed in nonviolence not only as a tactic but also as a creed or way of life. Such people possessed an inner strength and firm self-discipline that would not allow them to strike back, or, in McNamara's apt words, to appear as "an uncontrolled mob . . . frightening but ineffective." When Thoreau coined the term "civil resistance," he did not appear from the tone or substance of his essay to understand all the implications of that crucial term "civil," but Gandhi comprehended its manifold meanings for both the movement and its adversary, turning the concept of civility into a doctrine.*

CIVILITY

Civility, good manners and humility—these virtues are at such discount these days that they seem to have no place at all in the building of our character. . . .

Civility and humility are expressions of the spirit of non-violence while incivility and insolence indicates the spirit of violence. A non-co-operator, therefore, ought never to be uncivil. However, the most persistent charge leveled against non-co-operators is that they lack manners and are insolent, and the charge has much substance in it. We are apt to believe that in becoming non-co-operators we have done something very great, as if a person who had done no more than pay his debt had thereby become entitled to get an address [i.e., commendation].

This lack of manners delays our victory in the struggle we are carrying on, for, as politeness disarms anger and hatred, incivility increases hostility. Had non-co-operators remained courteous towards those who co-operated with the Government, had they, instead of abusing the latter, shown respect towards them, the existing bitterness between the two would not be there and the unhappy events [riots of November 1921] which were witnessed in Bombay would not have taken place. A student who has left his Government school should not harass or abuse another who may not have left his but should try, instead, to win him over with love. He should continue to render him the same service as he used to do before. A lawyer who has given up practice should not turn up his nose at another who may not have done so, but should maintain with him the same cordial relations as before. A person who has resigned from Government service should not run down another who may not have left it.

Had we, right from the beginning, approached our task in this spirit, it is possible that we would have reached our goal by now and the country would have advanced much further than it has done. The Moderate party would not then have kept away from us.

I trust no one will understand politeness to mean flattery. Nor does it mean hiding our regard for our dharma. To be polite means to show respect towards others while clinging to our own dharma. Because I put a vermilion mark [of Hindu faith] on my forehead, I may not sneer at another who does not do so. If I face the east when praying, I should not feel contempt for my Muslim brother who says his *namaz* [prayers] with his face towards the west. Ability to pronounce Sanskrit words correctly does not entitle me to speak contemptuously of the sounds in the Arabic language. A lover of khadi,* while wearing a khadi cap himself, can still be tolerant of a person who wears a sola hat and love him. If a man all clad in khadi starts swearing at a person wearing garments of foreign cloth, he will be acting as the most effective propagandist of such cloth. The incidents in Bombay have not made khadi more popular. On the contrary, it now stinks in the nostrils of some.

If we, khadi–lovers, wish to see the whole of India wearing khadi, we should patiently plead with people who used foreign cloth. However much we speak against such cloth, we should display nothing but love for those who use it. The plague is a dreadful disease but we, too, are likely to catch it if we turn away from any person who has got it. We may desire the disease to be rooted out but not the patient to be killed. If we look upon wearing foreign cloth as a kind of disease, we should attend on a person who suffers from it. May not a person who wears foreign cloth look upon us as the victims of a disease? By all means, let him do so. If, nonetheless, we continue to give our services to each other, sooner or later we shall discover which of us was in error. If we do not act in this way, we shall never discover the difference between what is dharma and what is *adharma*.

Just as it is necessary for us to be courteous to those who co-operate with the Government, so those of us who are imprisoned will also have to behave with civility in the prison. It is difficult to observe jail rules and yet maintain one's self-respect. Some of these rules are naturally humiliating. For instance, we have no choice but to let ourselves be confined in a cell. We must, thus, respect the rules which apply to all prisoners. At the same time, we should firmly oppose any measure which is intended merely to humiliate us. Once we have taught ourselves to behave with courtesy, we shall instinctively know how to act in a particular situation.

Where there is egotism, we shall find incivility and arrogance. Where it is absent, we shall find a sense of self-respect together with civility. The egotist thinks too much of his body. The man of self-respect recognizes the *atman* [self], is ever thinking about it and, in order to realize it, is always ready to sacrifice his body. He who holds his self-respect dear acts towards everyone in a spirit of friendship, for he values others' self-respect

*Homespun cotton cloth, here signifying commitment to the independence movement.

as much as he values his own. He sees himself in all and everyone else in himself,* puts himself in line with others. The egotist keeps aloof from others and, believing himself superior to the rest of the world, he takes upon himself to judge everyone and in the result enables the world to have the measure of his smallness.

Hence, the non-violent non-co-operator should regard civility as a distinct virtue and try to cultivate it. The importance attached to it provides the measure of an individual's or a nation's culture. A non-co-operator should realize very clearly that incivility is another name for brutishness and eschew it completely.[20]

THE NEED FOR HUMILITY

The spirit of non-violence necessarily leads to humility. Non-violence means reliance on God, the Rock of ages. If we would seek His aid, we must approach Him with a humble and a contrite heart. Non-co-operationists may not trade upon their amazing success at the Congress [in December 1920]. We must act, even as the mango tree which droops as it bears fruit. Its grandeur lies in its majestic lowliness. But one hears of non-co-operationists being insolent and intolerant in their behavior towards those who differ from them. I know that they will lose all their majesty and glory if they betray any inflation. . . .

Non-co-operation is not a movement of brag, bluster, or bluff. It is a test of our sincerity. It requires solid and silent self-sacrifice. It challenges our honesty and our capacity for national work. It is a movement that aims at translating ideas into action. And the more we do, the more we find that much more must be done than we had expected. And this thought of our imperfection must make us humble.

A non-co-operationist strives to compel attention and to set an example not by his violence but by his unobtrusive humility. He allows his solid action to speak for his creed. His strength lies in his reliance upon the correctness of his position. And the conviction of it grows most in his opponent when he least interposes his speech between his action and his opponent. Speech, especially when it is haughty, betrays want of confidence and it makes one's opponent skeptical about the reality of the act itself. Humility therefore is the key to quick success. I hope that every non-co-operationist will recognize the necessity of being humble and self-restrained.[21]

*As noted in the Introduction, Gandhi often invokes from *The Bhagavad-Gita* this concept of the universal self.

Thoughtless disobedience means disruption of society. The first thing therefore for those who aspire after civil disobedience is to learn the art of willingly obeying laws of voluntary associations such as congresses, conferences and other bodies and similarly obeying the state laws whether they like them or not. Civil disobedience is not a state of lawlessness and license, but presupposes a law-abiding spirit combined with self-restraint.[22]

The basic distinctions that Gandhi made between satyagraha *and passive resistance were suggested in the Introduction. The following articles elaborate on these differences. As we have just seen, a* satyagrahi *should always possess civility and humility, qualities that indicated self-control and an humble approach to truth. Gandhi's fundamental position on the idea of truth, that one must always be in pursuit of it and not claim possession of it, is clear from his statement opening the next article that "satyagraha . . . excludes the use of violence because man is not capable of knowing the absolute truth and, therefore, not competent to punish."*

Gandhi characterized civil disobedience as a "branch of satyagraha," and distinguished it from noncooperation, another branch, which he conceived as a mass refusal to obey government authority. Civil disobedience, he says, should be "practiced only as a last resort and [initially] by a select few," because it implies not only a refusal to comply (a mass strike), but an active targeting and deliberate flouting of laws to disobey. These distinctions appear in articles included here on the noncooperation campaign of 1919–22 in contrast to the civil disobedience movement of 1930–31.

The chief contrast that Gandhi wants to make here, however, is between satyagraha *and passive resistance. The latter avoids physical violence only because circumstances indicate it won't work. Not principle but expediency matters. Because nonviolence is not accepted as a creed, the resister may despise the adversary and easily give way to indiscipline or incivility. Gandhi also called this approach* duragraha, *action that is nonviolent in form but not in substance because it aims with flawed means at attaining a selfish goal. Hate speech or bias crimes may not be physically violent, but the harm they inflict through verbal assault constitutes* duragraha.

SATYAGRAHA, CIVIL DISOBEDIENCE, PASSIVE RESISTANCE, NON-CO-OPERATION

Satyagraha, then, is literally holding on to Truth and it means, therefore, Truth-force. Truth is soul or spirit. It is, therefore, known as soul-force. It excludes the use of violence because man is not capable of knowing the absolute truth and, therefore, not competent to punish. The word was coined in South Africa [in 1908] to distinguish the non-violent resistance of the Indians of South Africa from the contemporary "passive resistance" of the suffragettes and others. It is not conceived as a weapon of the weak.

Passive resistance is used in the orthodox English sense and covers the suffragette movement as well as the resistance of the nonconformists. Passive resistance has been conceived and is regarded as a weapon of the weak. Whilst it avoids violence, being not open to the weak, it does not exclude its use if, in the opinion of a passive resister, the occasion demands it. However, it has always been distinguished from armed resistance and its application was at one time confined to Christian martyrs.

Civil disobedience is civil breach of unmoral statutory enactments. The expression was, so far as I am aware, coined by Thoreau to signify his own resistance to the laws of a slave state. He has left a masterly treatise on the duty of civil disobedience. But Thoreau was not perhaps an out-and-out champion of non-violence. Probably, also, Thoreau limited his breach of statutory laws to the revenue law, i.e., payment of taxes, whereas the term "civil disobedience" as practiced in 1919 covered a breach of any statutory and unmoral law. It signified the resister's outlawry in a civil, i.e., non-violent manner. He invoked the sanctions of the law and cheerfully suffered imprisonment. It is a branch of satyagraha.

Non-co-operation predominantly implies withdrawing of co-operation from the state that in the non-co-operator's view has become corrupt and excludes civil disobedience of the fierce type described above. By its very nature, non-co-operation is even open to children of understanding and can be safely practiced by the masses. Civil disobedience presupposes the habit of willing obedience to laws without fear of their sanctions. It can therefore be practiced only as a last resort and by a select few in the first instance at any rate. Non-co-operation, too, like civil disobedience is a branch of satyagraha which includes all non-violent resistance for the vindication of Truth.[23]

SATYAGRAHA—NOT PASSIVE RESISTANCE

The force denoted by the term "passive resistance" and translated into Hindi as *nishkriya pratirodha* is not very accurately described either by the original English phrase or by its Hindi rendering. Its correct description is "satyagraha." Satyagraha was born in South Africa in 1908. There was no word in any Indian language denoting the power which our countrymen in South Africa invoked for the redress of their grievances. There was an English equivalent, namely, "passive resistance," and we carried on with it. However, the need for a word to describe this unique power came to be increasingly felt, and it was decided to award a prize to anyone who could think of an appropriate term. A Gujarati-speaking gentleman submitted the word "satyagraha," and it was adjudged the best.

"Passive resistance" conveyed the idea of the Suffragette Movement in England. Burning of houses by these women was called "passive resistance" and so also their fasting in prison. All such acts might very well be "passive resistance" but they were not "satyagraha." It is said of "passive resistance" that it is the weapon of the weak, but the power which is the subject of this article can be used only by the strong. This power is not "passive" resistance; indeed it calls for intense activity. The movement in South Africa was not passive but active. The Indians of South Africa believed that Truth was their object, that Truth ever triumphs, and with this definiteness of purpose they persistently held on to Truth. They put up with all the suffering that this persistence implied. With the conviction that Truth is not to be renounced even unto death, they shed the fear of death. In the cause of Truth, the prison was a palace to them and its doors the gateway to freedom.

Satyagraha is not physical force. A satyagrahi does not inflict pain on the adversary; he does not seek his destruction. A satyagrahi never resorts to firearms. In the use of satyagraha, there is no ill-will whatever.

Satyagraha is pure soul-force. Truth is the very substance of the soul. That is why this force is called satyagraha. The soul is informed with knowledge. In it burns the flame of love. If someone gives us pain through ignorance, we shall win him through love. "Non-violence is the supreme dharma" is the proof of this power of love. Non-violence is a dormant state. In the waking state, it is love. Ruled by love, the world goes on. In English there is a saying, "Might is Right." Then there is the doctrine of the survival of the fittest. Both of these ideas are contradictory to the above principle. Neither is wholly true. If ill-will were the chief motive-force, the world would have been destroyed long ago; and neither would I have had the opportunity to write this article nor would the hopes of the readers be fulfilled. We are alive solely because of love. We are ourselves the proof of this. Deluded by modern western civilization, we have forgotten our ancient civilization and worship the might of arms.

We forget the principle of non-violence, which is the essence of all religions. The doctrine of arms stands for irreligion. It is due to the sway of that doctrine that a sanguinary war is raging in Europe.

In India also we find worship of arms. We see it even in that great work of Tulsidas. But it is seen in all the books that soul-force is the supreme power. . . .

It brings good both to the satyagrahi and his adversary. It is ever victorious. For instance, Harishchandra was a satyagrahi, Prahlad was a satyagrahi, Mirabai was a satyagrahi. Daniel, Socrates and those Arabs who hurled themselves on the fire of the French artillery were all satyagrahis. We see from these examples that a satyagrahi does not fear for his body, he does not give up what he thinks is Truth; the word "defeat" is not to be found in his dictionary, he does not wish for the destruction of his antagonist, he does not vent anger on him; but has only compassion for him.

A satyagrahi does not wait for others, but throws himself into the fray, relying entirely on his own resources. He trusts that when the time comes, others will do likewise. His practice is his precept. Like air, satyagraha is all-pervading. It is infectious, which means that all people—big and small, men and women—can become satyagrahis. No one is kept out from the army of satyagrahis. A satyagrahi cannot perpetrate tyranny on anyone; he is not subdued through application of physical force; he does not strike at anyone. Just as anyone can resort to satyagraha, it can be resorted to in almost any situation.

People demand historical evidence in support of satyagraha. History is for the most part a record of armed activities. Natural activities find very little mention in it. Only uncommon activities strike us with wonder. Satyagraha has been used always and in all situations. The father and the son, the man and the wife are perpetually resorting to satyagraha, one towards the other. When a father gets angry and punishes the son, the son does not hit back with a weapon, he conquers his father's anger by submitting to him. The son refuses to be subdued by the unjust rule of his father but he puts up with the punishment that he may incur through disobeying the unjust father. We can similarly free ourselves of the unjust rule of the Government by defying the unjust rule and accepting the punishments that go with it. We do not bear malice towards the Government. When we set its fears at rest, when we do not desire to make armed assaults on the administrators, nor to unseat them from power, but only to get rid of their injustice, they will at once be subdued to our will.

The question is asked why we should call any rule unjust. In saying so, we ourselves assume the function of a judge. It is true. But in this world, we always have to act as judges for ourselves. That is why the satyagrahi does not strike his adversary with arms. If he has Truth on his side, he will win, and if his thought is faulty, he will suffer the consequences of his fault.

What is the good, they ask, of only one person opposing injustice; for he will be punished and destroyed, he will languish in prison or meet an untimely end through hanging. The objection is not valid. History shows that all reforms have begun with one person. Fruit is hard to come by without *tapasya* [self-sacrifice]. The suffering that has to be undergone in satyagraha is *tapasya* in its purest form. Only when the *tapasya* is capable of bearing fruit, do we have the fruit. This establishes the fact that when there is insufficient *tapasya*, the fruit is delayed. The *tapasya* of Jesus Christ, boundless though it was, was not sufficient for Europe's need. Europe has disapproved Christ. Through ignorance, it has disregarded Christ's pure way of life. Many Christs will have to offer themselves as sacrifice at the terrible altar of Europe, and only then will realization dawn on that continent. But Jesus will always be the first among these. He has been the sower of the seeds and his will therefore be the credit for raising the harvest.

It is said that it is a very difficult, if not an altogether impossible, task to educate ignorant peasants in satyagraha and that it is full of perils, for it is a very arduous business to transform unlettered ignorant people from one condition into another. Both the arguments are just silly. The people of India are perfectly fit to receive the training of satyagraha. India has knowledge of dharma [religious duty], and where there is knowledge of dharma, satyagraha is a very simple matter. The people of India have drunk of the nectar of devotion. This great people overflows with faith. It is no difficult matter to lead such a people on the right path of satyagraha. Some have a fear that once people get involved in satyagraha, they may at a later stage take to arms. This fear is illusory. From the path of satyagraha [clinging to Truth], a transition to the path of a-satyagraha [clinging to untruth] is impossible. It is possible of course that some people who believe in armed activity may mislead the satyagrahis by infiltrating into their ranks and later making them take to arms. This is possible in all enterprises. But as compared to other activities, it is less likely to happen in satyagraha, for their motives soon get exposed and when the people are not ready to take up arms, it becomes almost impossible to lead them on to that terrible path. The might of arms is directly opposed to the might of satyagraha. Just as darkness does not abide in light, soulless armed activity cannot enter the sunlike radiance of soul-force. Many Pathans took part in satyagraha in South Africa abiding by all the rules of satyagraha.

Then it is said that much suffering is involved in being a satyagrahi and that the entire people will not be willing to put up with this suffering. The objection is not valid. People in general always follow in the footsteps of the noble. There is no doubt that it is difficult to produce a satyagrahi leader. Our experience is that a satyagrahi needs many more virtues like self-control, fearlessness, etc., than are requisite for one who believes in armed action. The greatness of the man bearing arms does not lie in the superiority of the arms, nor does it lie in his physical prowess. It lies in his determination and fearlessness in face of death. . . . The strength of a warrior is not measured by reference to his weapons but by his firmness of mind. A satyagrahi needs millions of times more of such firmness than does a bearer of arms. The birth of such a man can bring about the salvation of India in no time. Not only India but the whole world awaits the advent of such a man. We may in the meanwhile prepare the ground as much as we can through satyagraha. . . .

For swaraj, satyagraha is the unfailing weapon. Satyagraha means that what we want is truth, that we deserve it and that we will work for it even unto death. . . .

Truth alone triumphs. There is no dharma [religion] higher than Truth. Truth always wins. We pray to God that in this sacred land we may bring about the reign of dharma by following satyagraha and that thus our country may become an example for all to follow.[24]

There are two methods of attaining one's goal. Satyagraha and *duragraha*. In our scriptures, they have been described, respectively, as divine and devilish modes of action. In satyagraha, there is always unflinching adherence to truth. It is never to be forsaken on any account. Even for the sake of one's country, it does not permit resort to falsehood. It proceeds on the assumption of the ultimate triumph of truth. A satyagrahi does not abandon his path, even though at times it seems impenetrable and beset with difficulties and dangers, and a slight departure from that straight path may appear full of promise. Even in these circumstances, his faith shines resplendent like the midday sun and he does not despond. With truth for his sword, he needs neither a steel sword nor gunpowder. Even an inveterate enemy he conquers by the force of the soul, which is love. Love for a friend is not put to the test. There is nothing surprising in a friend loving a friend; there is no merit in it and it costs no effort. When love is bestowed on the so-called enemy, it is tested, it becomes a virtue and requires an effort, and hence it is an act of manliness and real bravery. We can cultivate such an attitude even towards the Government and, doing so, we shall be able to appreciate their beneficial activities and, as for their errors, rather than feel bitter on their account, point them out in love and so get them rectified. Love does not act through fear. Weakness there certainly cannot be. A coward is incapable of bearing love, it is the prerogative of the brave. Looking at everything with love, we shall not regard the Government with suspicion, nor believe that all their actions are inspired with bad motives. And our examination of their actions, being directed by love, will be unerring and is bound, therefore, to carry conviction with them.

Love can fight; often it is obliged to. In the intoxication of power, man fails to see his error. When that happens, a satyagrahi does not sit still. He suffers. He disobeys the ruler's orders and his laws in a civil manner, and willingly submits to the penalties of such disobedience, for instance, imprisonment and gallows. Thus is the soul disciplined. In this, one never finds that one's time has been wasted and, if it is subsequently realized that such respectful disobedience was an error, the consequences are suffered merely by the satyagrahi and his co-workers. In the event, no bitterness develops between the satyagrahi and those in power; the latter, on the contrary, willingly yield to him. *They discover that they cannot command the satyagrahi's obedience. They cannot make him do anything against his will. And this is the consummation of swaraj, because it means complete independence.* It need not be assumed that such resistance is possible only against civilized rulers. Even a heart of flint will melt in the fire kindled by the power of the soul. Even a Nero becomes a lamb when he faces love. This is no exaggeration. It is as true as an algebraic equation. This satyagraha is India's distinctive weapon. It has had others but satyagraha has been in greater use. It is an unfailing source of strength, and is capable of being used at all times and under all circumstances. It requires no stamp of approval from the Congress or any other body. He who knows its power cannot but use it. Even as the eyelashes automatically protect the eyes, so does satyagraha, when kindled, automatically protect the freedom of the soul.

But *duragraha* is a force with the opposite attributes. . . . The man who follows the path of *duragraha* becomes impatient and wants to kill the so-called enemy. There can be but one result of this. Hatred increases. The defeated party vows vengeance and simply bides its time. The spirit of revenge thus descends from father to son. It is much to be wished that India never give predominance to this spirit of *duragraha*. If the members of this assembly deliberately accept satyagraha and chalk out its program accordingly, they will reach their goal all the more easily for doing so. They may have to face disappointment in the initial stages. They may not see results for a time. But satyagraha will triumph in the end. The *duragrahi*, like the oilman's ox, moves in a circle. His movement is only motion but it is not progress. The satyagrahi is ever moving forward. . . .

The right thing to hope from India is that this great and holy Aryan land will ever give the predominant place to the divine force and employ the weapon of satyagraha, that it will never accept the supremacy of armed strength. India will never respect the principle of might being right. She will ever reserve her allegiance to the principle: "Truth alone triumphs." On reflection, we find that we can employ satyagraha even for social reform. We can rid ourselves of the many defects of our caste system. We can resolve Hindu–Muslim differences and we can solve political problems. It is all right that, for the sake of convenience, we speak of these things as separate subjects. But it should never be forgotten that they are all closely inter-related. It is not true to say that neither religion nor social reform has anything to do with politics.[25]

_____

In the excerpt from Jawaharlal Nehru's Discovery of India quoted in the Introduction, the political situation in India before Gandhi's rise to power seemed desperate, even hopeless. The freedom struggle, begun in 1885, had stalled thirty years later from a lack of will and imagination. The country's condition was dramatically transformed in the spring of 1919 when under Gandhi's leadership a mass movement was born. From April 6, 1919, when "Satyagraha Day" was observed throughout India to initiate nonviolent action, to August 1, 1920, when a second stage of noncooperation began by announcing a systematic and prolonged attack on the Raj, Gandhi's method was tested. It succeeded beyond anyone's expectations, Indian or British. The first article that follows refers to this period.

Most surprising was how the villages of India were mobilized through an unprecedented combination of leadership, ideology, and organization. Before Gandhi's emergence, the Indian Congress had produced magnificent oratory and sophisticated leaders, but it utterly lacked a mass base. Gandhi's achievement at the helm of the Congress understandably alarmed the British authorities, both in England and in India. A committee to investigate the "disorders" was appointed. A sampling of Gandhi's testimony before this committee is included, which he gave two years before he was arrested for sedition and imprisoned in March 1922. His defense indicates how firmly he feels that he has captured the moral high ground of the struggle. He argues the movement's devotion to absolute nonviolence, pursuit of truth, and even to the constitutional nature of satyagraha because of its commitment to a higher law.

Much has been made of Gandhi's admission in the article here, entitled "Doctrine of the Sword," that he would prefer violence to cowardice or to India's living in a perpetual state of fearful submission. His main point, however, is that nonviolence is always superior to violence, as he makes clear at the end of this article. But satyagraha must be learned and applied through discipline and devotion to truth.

_____

THE FIRST OF AUGUST

It must be clear to anyone that the power that wrests justice from an un-willing Government . . . is the power of satyagraha whether it is known by the name of civil disobedience or non-co-operation.

Many people dread the advent of non-co-operation, because of the events of last year. They fear madness from the mob and consequent rep-etition of last year's reprisals almost unsurpassed in their ferocity in the history of modern times. Personally I do not mind Governmental fury as I mind mob fury. The latter is a sign of national distemper and therefore more difficult to deal with than the former which is confined to a small corporation. It is easier to oust a Government that has rendered itself un-fit to govern than it is to cure unknown people in a mob of their madness. But great movements cannot be stopped altogether because a Govern-ment or a people or both go wrong. We learn to profit from our mistakes and failures. And so we must approach non-co-operation with confidence and hope. As in the past, the commencement is to be marked by fasting and prayer as a sign of the religious character of the demonstration. There should also be on that day suspension of business, and meetings to pass resolutions. . . .

But the greatest thing in this campaign of non-co-operation is to evolve order, discipline, co-operation among the people, co-ordination among the workers. Effective non-co-operation depends upon complete organi-zation. Thousands of men who have filled meetings throughout the Pun-jab have convinced me that the people want to withdraw co-operation from the Government but they must know how. Most people do not understand the complicated machinery of the Government. They do not realize that every citizen silently but nonetheless certainly sustains the Government of the day in ways of which he has no knowledge. Every citizen therefore renders himself responsible for every act of this Government. And it is quite proper to support it so long as the actions of the Government are bearable. But when they hurt him and his nation, it becomes his duty to withdraw his support.

But as I have said, every citizen does not know how to do so in an or-derly manner. Disorderliness comes from anger, orderliness out of intelli-gent resistance. The first condition therefore of real success is to ensure entire absence of violence. Violence done to persons representing the Government or to persons who do not join our ranks, i.e., the supporters of the Government, means in every case retrogression in our case, cessa-tion of non-co-operation and useless waste of innocent lives. Those there-

fore who wish to make non-co-operation a success in the quickest possible
time will consider it their first duty to see that in their neighborhood complete order is kept.[26]

. . . We need perfect discipline and training in voluntary obedience to
be able to offer civil disobedience. Civil disobedience is the active expression of non-violence. Civil disobedience distinguishes the non-violence of
the strong from the passive, i.e., negative non-violence of the weak. And
as weakness cannot lead to swaraj, negative non-violence must fail to
achieve our purpose.

Have we then the requisite discipline? Have we, a friend asked me,
evolved the spirit of obedience to our own rules and resolutions? Whilst
we have made tremendous headway during the past twelve months, we
have certainly not made enough to warrant us in embarking upon civil
disobedience with easy confidence. Rules voluntarily passed by us and
rules which carry no sanction save the disapproval of our own conscience
must be like debts of honor held far more binding than rules superim-
posed upon us or rules whose breach we can purge by paying the penalty
thereof. It follows that if we have not learnt the discipline of obeying our
own rules, in other words carrying out our own promises, we are ill-
adapted for disobedience that can be at all described as civil. I do therefore
suggest to every Congressman, every non-co-operator, and above all to
every member of the All-India Congress Committee to set himself or herself right with the Congress and his or her creed by carrying on the
strictest self-examination and by correcting himself or herself wherever
he or she might have failed.[27]

THE NON-CO-OPERATION RESOLUTION

This Congress is of [the] opinion that there can be no contentment in
India without . . . progressive non-violent non-co-operation . . . and swa-
rajya is established.

And inasmuch as a beginning should be made by the classes who have
hitherto molded and represented opinion and inasmuch as Government
consolidates its power through titles and honors bestowed on the people,
through schools controlled by it, its law-courts and its legislative councils,
and inasmuch as it is desirable in the prosecution of the movement to take
the minimum risk and to call for the least sacrifice compatible with the attainment of the desired object, this Congress earnestly advises

(a) surrender of titles and honorary offices and resignation from nom-
inated seats in local bodies;

(b) refusal to attend Government levees, durbars, and other official and semi-official functions held by Government officials or in their honor;

(c) gradual withdrawal of children from schools and colleges owned, aided or controlled by Government and in place of such schools and colleges establishment of national schools and colleges in various Provinces;

(d) gradual boycott of British courts by lawyers and litigants and establishment of private arbitration courts by their aid for the settlement of private disputes;

(e) refusal on the part of the military, clerical and laboring classes to offer themselves as recruits for service in Mesopotamia;

(f) withdrawal by candidates of their candidature for election to the reformed councils and refusal on the part of the voters to vote for any candidate who may despite the Congress advice offer himself for election;

(g) the boycott of foreign goods.

And inasmuch as non-co-operation has been conceived as a measure of discipline and self-sacrifice without which no nation can make real progress, and inasmuch as an opportunity should be given in the very first stage of non-co-operation to every man, woman, and child, for such discipline and self-sacrifice, this Congress advises adoption of swadeshi in piece-goods on a vast scale, and inasmuch as the existing mills of India with indigenous capital and control do not manufacture sufficient yarn and sufficient cloth for the requirements of the nation, and are not likely to do so for a long time to come, this Congress advises immediate stimulation of further manufacture on a large scale by means of reviving hand-spinning in every home and hand-weaving on the part of the millions of weavers who have abandoned their ancient and honorable calling for want of encouragement.[28]

EVIDENCE BEFORE DISORDERS INQUIRY COMMITTEE*

Mr. Gandhi, we have been informed that you are the author of the satyagraha movement?

Yes, sir.

I would like to give you an explanation of what that movement is.

*The Disorders Inquiry Committee, convened to investigate Gandhi's movement, was presided over by Lord Hunter. The committee consisted of Justice Rankin, W. F. Rice, Major-General Sir George Barrow, Jagat Narayan, Thomas Smith, Sir C. H. Setalvad, and Sultan Ahmad Khan, with N. Williamson as secretary. Brigadier-General Dyer appeared before the Committee at Lahore.

It is a movement intended to replace methods of violence. It is a movement based entirely on truth. It is, as I have conceived it, an extension of the domestic law on the political field, and my own experience has led me to the conclusion that that movement and that movement alone can rid India of the possibilities of violence spreading throughout the length and breadth of the land for the redress of grievances, supposed or real. . . .

For the past thirty years I have been preaching and practicing satyagraha. The principles of satyagraha, as I know it today, constitute a gradual evolution.

Satyagraha differs from passive resistance as North Pole from South. The latter has been conceived as a weapon of the weak and does not exclude the use of physical force or violence for the purpose of gaining one's end, whereas the former has been conceived as a weapon of the strongest and excludes the use of violence in any shape or form.

The term satyagraha was coined by me in South Africa to express the force that the Indians there used for a full eight years and it was coined in order to distinguish it from the movement then going on in the United Kingdom and South Africa under the name of passive resistance.

Its root meaning is holding on to truth, hence truth-force. I have also called it love-force or soul-force. In the application of satyagraha, I discovered in the earliest stages that pursuit of truth did not admit of violence being inflicted on one's opponent but that he must be weaned from error by patience and sympathy. For what appears to be truth to the one may appear to be error to the other. And patience means self-suffering. So the doctrine came to mean vindication of truth, not by infliction of suffering on the opponent, but on one's self.

But on the political field, the struggle on behalf of the people mostly consists in opposing error in the shape of unjust laws. When you have failed to bring the error home to the law-giver by way of petitions and the like, the only remedy open to you, if you do not wish to submit to error, is to compel him by physical force to yield to you or by suffering in your own person by inviting the penalty for the breach of the law. Hence satyagraha largely appears to the public as civil disobedience or civil resistance. It is civil in the sense that it is not criminal.

The law-breaker breaks the law surreptitiously and tries to avoid the penalty; not so the civil resister. He ever obeys the laws of the State to which he belongs not out of fear of the sanctions but because he considers them to be good for the welfare of society. But there come occasions, generally rare, when he considers certain laws to be so unjust as to render obedience to them a dishonor. He then openly and civilly breaks them and quietly suffers the penalty for their breach. And in order to register his protest against the action of the law-givers, it is open to him to withdraw his co-operation from the State by disobeying such other laws whose breach does not involve moral turpitude.

In my opinion, the beauty and efficacy of satyagraha are so great and the doctrine so simple that it can be preached even to children. It was preached by me to thousands of men, women and children commonly called indentured Indians, with excellent results.

When the Rowlatt Bills were published I felt that they were so restrictive of human liberty that they must be resisted to the utmost. I observed too that the opposition to them was universal among Indians. I submit that no State however despotic has the right to enact laws which are repugnant to the whole body of the people, much less a government guided by constitutional usage and precedent such as the Indian Government. I felt too that the oncoming agitation needed a definite direction if it was neither to collapse nor to run into violent channels.

I ventured therefore to present satyagraha to the country emphasizing its civil resistance aspect. And as it is purely an inward and purifying movement, I suggested the observance of fast, prayer and suspension of all work for one day—the 6th of April [1919]. There was a magnificent response throughout the length and breadth of India, even in little villages, although there was no organization and no great previous preparation. The idea was given to the public as soon as it was conceived. On the 6th April there was no violence used by the people and no collision with the police worth naming. The hartal was purely voluntary and spontaneous. . . .

Was it your intention to enlist as many satyagrahis as possible?

Yes, consistently with the carrying on of the movement in a proper way, that is to say, if I found a million men who were capable of understanding the truth and adhering by it and never using violence, I would certainly be glad to have the million men. . . .

I suppose it is the case in India as elsewhere that people differ as to the justice or injustice of particular laws?

Yes; and that is the reason, the main reason, why violence is eliminated here. The satyagrahi gives his opponent the same right of independence and feeling of truth that he reserves to himself, seeing that [if] he wants to fight for truth he will do so by inviting injury upon his own person. . . .

Is not refusing to obey that or any other law you choose to select a rather drastic way of attempting to do that?

I respectfully differ. When I find that even my father has imposed upon me a law which is repugnant to my conscience, I think it is the least drastic course that I adopt by respectfully telling him, "Father, I cannot obey this." I do nothing but justice to my father when I do that. If I may say so without any disrespect to the Committee, I have simply followed that in my own domestic circle, and I found I had done so with the greatest advantage. I have placed that before Indians and everybody for acceptance. Rather than feel angry with my father, I would respectfully tell him, "I cannot obey this law." I see nothing wrong in that. If it is not wrong for me to say so to my father, there is nothing wrong for me to say so to a friend or to a Government. . . .

Do you not create a condition of very great danger to peace and order?

On the contrary, I promote peace. And I have done it myself on the 6th of April, because I was there in Bombay, and there was some fear of people themselves offering violence. And I am here to tell you that no violence, no real violence was offered by the people, because people were being told the true nature of satyagraha. It was an amazing sight for me to see thousands of people behaving in a perfectly peaceful manner. That would not have been the case if the satyagraha doctrine had not been preached in the right key. . . .

In Ahmedabad . . . your arrest seems to have created a great resentment on their part, and very unfortunately again, on the part of the mob. . . .

I consider that the action of this mob, whether in Ahmedabad or in Viramgam, was totally unjustified, and I have thought that it was a very sad thing that they lost self-control. I do not wish to offer the slightest defense for the acts of the mob, but at the same time I would like to say that the people amongst whom, rightly or wrongly, I was popular were put to such severe stress by Government who should have known better. I think the Government committed an unpardonable error of judgment and the mob committed a similar unpardonable error, but more unpardonable on the part of the mob than on the part of the Government. I wish to say that also as a satyagrahi, I cannot find a single thing done by the mob which I can defend or justify. No amount of provocation, however great, could justify people from doing as they have done. It has been suggested to me that all those who did it were not satyagrahis. That is true. But they chose to take part in the satyagraha movement and came under the satyagraha discipline. These were the terms in which I have spoken to the people; and it

gives me the greatest pleasure and also pain to declare my settled conviction before this Committee also.

With regard to your satyagraha doctrine, as far as I am able to understand it, it
involves a pursuit of truth?

Yes.

Now in that doctrine, who is to determine the truth? That individual himself?

Yes, that individual himself.

So each one that adopts this doctrine has to determine for himself what is the
truth that he will pursue?

Most decidedly.

And in doing that different individuals will take very different views as to what
is the truth to be pursued?

Certainly.

It might, on that footing, cause considerable confusion?

I won't accept that. It need not lead to any confusion if you accept the
proposition that a man is honestly in search after truth and that he will
never inflict violence upon him who holds to truth. Then there is no possibility of confusion.

A man may honestly strive after truth, but however honestly a man may
strive, his notions of truth will be quite different from the notions of truth
of some other people or his intellectual equipment may be of such a character that his conclusion as regards truth may be entirely opposite to the
conclusion of somebody else?

That was precisely the reason why in answer to Lord Hunter I suggested that non-violence was the necessary corollary to the acceptance of
satyagraha doctrine.[29]

IS IT UNCONSTITUTIONAL?

I have been told that non-co-operation is unconstitutional. I venture to
deny that it is unconstitutional. On the contrary, I hold that non-co-
operation is a just and religious doctrine; it is the inherent right of every
human being and it is perfectly constitutional. A great lover of the British
Empire has said that under the British Constitution, even a successful rebellion is perfectly constitutional and he quotes historical instances which

I cannot deny in support of his claim. I do not claim any constitutionality for a rebellion successful or otherwise so long as that rebellion means in the ordinary sense of the term what it does mean, namely, wresting justice by violent means. On the contrary, I have said it repeatedly to my countrymen that violence, whatever end it may serve in Europe, will never serve us in India. My brother and friend Shaukat Ali* believes in methods of violence; and if it was in his power to draw the sword against the British Empire, I know that he has got the courage of a man and he has got also the wisdom to see that he should offer that battle to the British Empire. But because he recognizes as a true soldier that means of violence are not open to India, he sides with me accepting my humble assistance and pledges his word that so long as I am with him and so long as he believes in the doctrine so long will he not harbor even the idea of violence against any single Englishman or any single man on earth. I am here to tell you that he has been as true as his word and has kept it religiously. I am here to bear witness that he has been following out this plan of non-violent non-co-operation to the very letter and I am asking India to follow this non-violent non-co-operation. I tell you that there is not a better soldier living in our ranks in British India than Shaukat Ali. When the time for the drawing of the sword comes, if it ever comes, you will find him drawing that sword and you will find me retiring to the jungle of Hindustan. As soon as India accepts the doctrine of the sword, my life as an Indian is finished. It is because I believe in a mission special to India, and it is because I believe that the ancients of India, after centuries of experience, have found out that the true thing for any human being on earth is not justice based on violence but justice based on sacrifice of self, justice based on *yajna* and *kurbani* [sacrifice]—I cling to that doctrine and I shall cling to it for ever—it is for that reason I tell you that whilst my friend believes also in the doctrine of violence and has adopted the doctrine of non-violence as a weapon of the weak, I believe in the doctrine of non-violence as a weapon of the strongest. I believe that a man is the strongest soldier for daring to die unarmed with his breast bare before the enemy. So much for the non-violent part of non-co-operation. I, therefore, venture to suggest to my learned countrymen that so long as the doctrine of non-co-operation remains non-violent so long there is nothing unconstitutional in the doctrine.

I ask further, is it unconstitutional for me to say to the British Government, "I refuse to serve you?" Is it unconstitutional for our worthy chairman to return with every respect all the titles that he has ever held from

*A principal Muslim leader within the nationalist movement.

the Government? Is it unconstitutional for any parent to withdraw his children from a Government or aided school? Is it unconstitutional for a lawyer to say, "I shall no longer support the arm of the law so long as that arm of law is used not to raise me but to debase me?" Is it unconstitutional for a civil servant or for a judge to say, "I refuse to serve a Government which does not wish to respect the wishes of the whole people?" I ask, is it unconstitutional for a policeman or for a soldier to tender his resignation when he knows that he is called to serve a Government which traduces its own countrymen? Is it unconstitutional for me to go to the "krishak," to the agriculturist, and say to him, "It is not wise for you to pay any taxes, if these taxes are used by the Government not to raise you but to weaken you?" I hold and venture to submit that there is nothing unconstitutional in it. What is more, I have done everyone of these things in my life and nobody has questioned the constitutional character of it. I was in Kaira working in the midst of seven lakhs of agriculturists. They had all suspended the payment of taxes and the whole of India was at one with me. Nobody considered that it was unconstitutional. I submit that in the whole plan of non-co-operation there is nothing unconstitutional. But I do venture to suggest that it will be highly unconstitutional in the midst of this unconstitutional Government—in the midst of a nation which has built up its magnificent constitution—for the people of India to become weak and to crawl on their belly*—it will be highly unconstitutional for the people of India to pocket every insult that is offered to them; it is highly unconstitutional for the 70 millions of Mohammedans of India to submit to a violent wrong done to their religion; it is highly unconstitutional for the whole of India to sit still and co-operate with an unjust Government which has trodden under its feet the honor of the Punjab; I say to my countrymen: "So long as you have a sense of honor and so long as you wish to remain the descendants and defenders of the noble traditions that have been handed to you for generations after generations, it is unconstitutional for you not to non-co-operate and unconstitutional for you to co-operate with a Government which has become so unjust as our government has become. I am not anti-English; I am not anti-British; I am not anti-any government; but I am anti-untruth—anti-humbug and anti-injustice. So long as the Government spells injustice, it may regard me as its enemy, implacable enemy. I had hoped at the Congress at Amritsar—I

---

*A reference to Dyer's infamous "crawling order" following the Amritsar massacre in April 1919. See *CWMG* 39: 375 for Gandhi's expression of outrage at this humiliation.

am speaking God's truth before you—when I pleaded on knees before some of you for co-operation with the Government, I had full hope that the British ministers, who are wise as a rule, would placate the Mussulman sentiment, that they would do full justice in the matter of the Punjab atrocities, and, therefore, I said: Let us return goodwill to the land of fellowship that has been extended to us, which, I then believed, was extended to us through the Royal Proclamation. It was on that account that I pleaded for co-operation. But today that faith having gone and [been] obliterated by the acts of the British ministers, I am here to plead not for futile obstruction in the legislative council but for real substantial non-cooperation which would paralyze the mightiest government on earth. That is what I stand for today. Until we have wrung justice and until we have wrung our self-respect from unwilling hands and from unwilling pens, there can be no co-operation. Our Shastras say and I say so with the greatest deference to all the greatest religious preceptors of India but without fear of contradiction that our Shastras teach us that there shall be no co-operation between injustice and justice, between an unjust man and a justice-loving man, between truth and untruth. Co-operation is a duty only so long as Government protects your honor, and non-co-operation is an equal duty when the Government, instead of protecting robs you of your honor. That is the doctrine of non-co-operation. . . .

I have suggested another difficult matter, viz, that the lawyers should suspend their practice. How should I do otherwise knowing so well how the Government had always been able to retain this power through the instrumentality of lawyers? It is perfectly true that it is the lawyers of today who are leading us, who are fighting the country's battles, but when it comes to a matter of action against the Government, when it comes to a matter of paralyzing the activity of the Government, I know that the Government always looks to the lawyers, however fine fighters they may have been, to preserve their dignity and their self-respect. I, therefore, suggest to my lawyer friends that it is their duty to suspend their practice and to show the Government that they will not longer retain their offices, because lawyers are considered to be honorary officers of the courts and, therefore, subject to their disciplinary jurisdiction. They must no longer retain these honorary offices if they want to withdraw co-operation from Government. But what will happen to law and order? We shall evolve law and order through the instrumentality of these very lawyers. We shall promote arbitration courts and dispense justice, pure, simple, home-made justice, swadeshi justice to our countrymen. That is what suspension of practice means.

I have suggested yet another difficulty—to withdraw our children from the Government schools and to ask collegiate students to withdraw from the college and to empty Government-aided schools. How could I do otherwise? I want to gauge the national sentiment. I want to know whether the Mohammedans feel deeply. If they feel deeply, they will understand in the twinkling of an eye that it is not right for them to receive schooling from a government in which they have lost all faith; and which they do not trust at all. How can I, if I do not want to help this Government, receive any help from that Government? I think that the schools and colleges are factories for making clerks and Government servants. I would not help this great factory for manufacturing clerks and servants if I want to withdraw co-operation from that Government. Look at it from any point of view you like. It is not possible for you to send your children to the schools and still believe in the doctrine of non-co-operation.

I have gone further. I have suggested that our title-holders should give up their titles. How can they hold on to the titles and honors bestowed by this Government? They were at one time badges of honor when we believed that national honor was safe in their hands. But now they are no longer badges of honor but badges of dishonor and disgrace when we really believe that we cannot get justice from this Government. Every title-holder holds his title and honors as trustee for the nation and in this first step in the withdrawal of co-operation from the Government, they should surrender their titles without a moment's consideration. . . .

You may consider that I have spoken these words in anger because I have considered the ways of this Government immoral, unjust, debasing and untruthful. I use these adjectives with the greatest deliberations. I have used them for my own true brother with whom I was engaged in a battle of non-co-operation for full thirteen years and although the ashes cover the remains of my brother, I tell you that I used to tell him that he was unjust when his plans were based upon immoral foundation. I used to tell him that he did not stand for truth. There was no anger in me. I told him this home truth because I loved him. In the same manner I tell the British people that I love them and that I want their association but I want that association on conditions well defined. I want my self-respect and I want my absolute equality with them. If I cannot gain the equality from the British people, I do not want the British connection. . . . It is for that reason I stand before you and implore you to offer this religious battle, but it is not a battle offered to you by a visionary or a saint. I deny being a visionary. I do not accept the claim of saintliness. I am of the earth, earthly, a common gardener man as much as anyone of you, probably much more than you are. I am prone to as many weaknesses as you are. But I have seen the world. I have lived in the world with my eyes open. I have gone through the most fiery ordeals that have fallen to the lot of man. I have gone through this discipline. I have understood the secret of my own sacred Hinduism. I have learnt the lesson that non-co-operation is the duty not merely of the saint but it is the duty of every ordinary citizen, who not knowing much, not caring to know much, but wants to perform his ordinary household functions. The people of Europe teach even their masses, the poor people, the doctrine of the sword. But the *rishis* of India, those who have held the traditions of India, have preached to the masses of India the doctrine, not of the sword, not of violence but of suffering, of self-suffering. And unless you and I are prepared to go through the primary lesson, we are not ready even to offer the sword and that is the lesson my brother Shaukat Ali has imbibed to teach and that is why he today accepts my advice tendered to him in all prayerfulness and in all humility and says: "Long live non-co-operation."[30]

DOCTRINE OF THE SWORD

I have no dearth of advisers. They send me letters, signed and unsigned, and some visit me to proffer their advice in person. Some write to me to say that I am a coward, afraid of the sword, and, therefore, I shall achieve nothing in this world; that it is my fear which makes me prate about non-violence without knowing what it means. Some others tell me that I have violence enough in my heart, that I approve of killing, but that I am such a "shrewd fellow" and so "cunning" that I do not let people know what I think and, though talking about non-violence, at heart want them to instigate violence. Besides these, there is another class of men who think that I am not a rogue but am only waiting for my opportunity and, when it comes, I shall advise people to use the sword. These people think that the time for this is ripe and that now I should wait no longer. . . .

Sword-force is brute force. Killing people requires no intelligence. We may, indeed, by misdirecting our intelligence employ it in the service of brute force, but, though aided by intelligence, brute force remains brute force and the law of the sword remains the law of the beast. In the latter, the self is in a state of nascence and can have no knowledge of itself. That is why we know the animal world as enveloped in darkness. The activities of eating, drinking, sleeping, feeling afraid, etc., are common to man and beast. But man has the power of distinguishing between good and evil and can also know the self. One animal subdues another simply by its physical might. Its world is ruled by that law, but not so the human world. The law which is most in harmony with human nature is that of winning over others by the power of love—by soul-force. When, therefore, a man wins over an enemy through love, he simply follows the law of his nature. He has not become a god in doing so. Gods have no physical body. They behave sometimes like beasts and sometimes like men. There are white gods as also black gods. Man is, at times, seen acting like an animal. He is endowed with brute force as well, and, so long as he has not developed awareness of his spiritual nature he remains an intelligent animal. Though human in body, instead of obeying the law of his kind he follows the law of the animal. This, however, should not be regarded as his true nature. I believe, therefore, that if we wake up to the consciousness of our true nature, we would, that very moment, renounce the law of the jungle.

But the sages saw that the passions of the beast had not died out in most persons, though they possessed human bodies. They recognized, therefore, that there was scope for the use of brute force even by human beings and showed under what circumstances it could be employed.

When a man submits to another through fear, he does not follow his nature but yields to brute force. He who has no desire to dominate others by brute force will not himself submit to such force either. Recognizing, therefore, that a man who fears brute force has not attained self-knowledge at all, our Shastras allowed him the use of brute force while he remains in this state.

A Pathan made a murderous attack on me in 1908. My eldest son [Harilal Gandhi] was not present then. He possessed fairly good physical strength. I did not have the Pathan prosecuted since I held the same views then as I do now. I was educating my sons too in the ideas of forgiveness and love, and so at our very first meeting [after the assault], my son said to me: "I want to know what my duty would have been if I had been with you at the time. You have taught us that we may not strike back or tamely submit to the other man. I understand this principle but I have not the strength to act upon it. I could not remain a silent spectator while you were being beaten to death. I would consider it my duty to protect you if you should be assaulted, but I could not do this by laying down my own life [instead of striking back]. I must, therefore, either protect you by attacking the man who would strike you, or be a passive witness to the attack on you, or run away." I told him: "It would be a sign of cowardice if you ran away or did nothing to protect me. If you could not protect me by taking the anger upon yourself, you should undoubtedly do so by attacking the other man. It is any day better to use brute force than to betray cowardice." I hold this view even now. It is better that India should arm itself and take the risk than that it should refuse to take up arms out of fear. . . . It will be evidence of India's soul-force only if it refuses to fight when it has the strength to do so.

It is necessary to understand what the phrase, "strength to fight" means in this context. It does not mean only physical strength. Everyone who has courage in him can have the strength to fight, and everyone who has given up fear of death has such strength. . . . Thus, the day India gives up fear we shall be able to say that she has the strength to fight. It is not at all true to say that, to be able to fight, it is essential to acquire the ability to use arms; the moment, therefore, a man wakes up the power of the soul, that very moment he comes to know the strength he has for fighting. . . .

To me, on the day when brute force gains ascendancy in India, all distinctions of East and West, of ancient and modern, will have disappeared. That day will be the day of my test. I take pride in looking upon India as my country because I believe that she has it in her to demonstrate to the world the supremacy of soul-force. When India accepts the supremacy of brute force, I should no longer be happy to call her my motherland. It is my belief that my dharma recognizes no limits of spheres of duty or of geographical boundaries. I pray to God that I may then be able to prove that my dharma takes no thought of my person or is not restricted to a particular field.[31]

The success of the noncooperation movement in 1921 prompted Gandhi to consider escalating nonviolent action to the higher stage of mass civil disobedience, but, as explained, the violent mob outburst at Chauri Chaura in early 1922 compelled him to stop the campaign. The first article in this section, dated August 1921, indicates that he always contemplated civil disobedience with extreme reluctance and tried to restrain those "impatient to embark" on it.

Gandhi was in prison from 1922 to 1924. After his release, he concentrated on the program of social reforms that he called "constructive work" and swadeshi. *This aimed at Hindu-Muslim unity, the abolition of untouchability, and the uplift of villages, especially through improvement of the handicraft industries like spinning of cotton cloth* (khadi). *These social reforms, he insisted, were prerequisites for* swaraj. *They are examined in Part II of the readings.*

In 1928, a local tax-resistance campaign in the western Indian district of Bardoli, Gujarat, proved successful. Gandhi found in this small-scale movement the key for his next national campaign, which in 1930 took the long-planned leap into mass civil disobedience. This historic action, easily the largest movement of civil disobedience ever undertaken, became known as the "salt satyagraha*" because it was a tax-resistance campaign aimed at the duty the government imposed on salt. The tax was the equivalent of forty-six cents on each* maund *(eighty-two-pound unit), which constituted 8.4 percent of the total revenue collected by the Raj. By Gandhi's calculation, the tax could constitute three days' income for the average villager.[32]*

Gandhi's letter to Lord Irwin, the Viceroy of India, is the second piece included in this section. It dwells on the economic burden that the salt tax imposed on the poor, but Gandhi knew that the real force of the salt satyagraha *came from its symbolic meaning. Once again, he found a way to seize the moral high ground by conveying a heroic struggle against a cruelly exploitative foreign system that, as he says in his letter to Irwin, "seems to be designed to crush the very life out of" its victims.*

This letter to Irwin surely represents Gandhi at his best, informing his adversary in advance of his intentions and reasons, even the details of his battle plans. Beginning in Gandhi's classic style with "Dear Friend," it sets the tone of congeniality and trust that served to create ambivalence in the British and make them hesitate, for them a fatal concession to the campaign. It is noteworthy that Gandhi's letter opens with a humble plea that the Viceroy help him "find a way out" so that disobedience would not be necessary. But there is of course power behind his plea, the power of what he later calls in his letter the "intensely active force" of nonviolence. His careful explanation in the bulk of the letter of precisely why he regards "British rule to be a curse" gives eloquent justification for civil disobedience.

The salt satyagraha *began on March 12, 1930. Gandhi, age sixty, commenced his march with eighty followers, from his ashram near Ahmedabad, traveling through his home state of Gujarat, bound for the village of Dandi, over two hundred miles away on the western seacoast of India. He reached his destination twenty-four days later, unhindered by the government. At 6:30 A.M. on April 6, he collected a handful of natural sea salt, its use prohibited by law because it was untaxed. Press reporters and film crews from the United States, Britain, and Europe who had determined that the Mahatma was newsworthy crowded around to record the event. He did not disappoint them, proclaiming to all the world: "With this I am shaking the foundations of the British Empire. . . . I want world sympathy in this battle of Right against Might. . . . That I have reached here is in no small measure due to the power of peace and non-violence: that power is universally felt."[33] The response was electric: mass civil disobedience throughout India followed as millions broke the salt laws, filling prisons and paralyzing the government. The viceroy had*

*clearly been mistaken by not arresting Gandhi at once because the delay
allowed the movement's quick escalation. By the time he was arrested on May
5, the momentum was unstoppable; it continued unabated until February–
March 1931, when Gandhi was released and concluded talks with Irwin. This
was the first time that these two leaders had negotiated on equal terms, and
from that point the independence of India became assured, signified by the
Government of India Act of 1935. When Time made Gandhi its "Man of
the Year" for 1930, it recognized the unique quality of the salt satyagraha:
never before had a nonviolent movement become a revolutionary event.*[34]

CIVIL DISOBEDIENCE

Civil disobedience was on the lips of every one of the members of the All-
India Congress Committee. Not having really ever tried it, everyone appeared to be enamored of it from a mistaken belief in it as a sovereign
remedy for our present-day ills. I feel sure that it can be made such if we
can produce the necessary atmosphere for it. For individuals there always
is that atmosphere except when their civil disobedience is certain to lead
to bloodshed. I discovered this exception during the satyagraha days. But
even so, a call may come which one dare not neglect, cost what it may. I
can clearly see the time coming to me when I must refuse obedience to
every single State-made law, even though there may be a certainty of
bloodshed. When neglect of the call means a denial of God, civil disobedience becomes a peremptory duty.

Mass civil disobedience stands on a different footing. It can only be
tried in a calm atmosphere. It must be the calmness of strength not weakness, of knowledge not ignorance. . . .

It was in a practically uninhabited tract of country that I was arrested in
South Africa when I was marching into prohibited area with over two to
three thousand men and some women.* The company included several
Pathans and others who were able-bodied men. It was the greatest testimony of merit the Government of South Africa gave to the movement.
They knew that we were as harmless as we were determined. It was easy
enough for that body of men to cut to pieces those who arrested me. It
would have not only been a most cowardly thing to do, but it would have
been a treacherous breach of their own pledge, and it would have meant
ruin to the struggle for freedom and the forcible deportation of every

*Gandhi was arrested in South Africa on November 6, 1913, while leading men,
women, and children into the Transvaal on their "Great March."

Indian from South Africa. But the men were no rabble. They were disciplined soldiers and all the better for being unarmed. Though I was torn from them, they did not disperse, nor did they turn back. They marched onto their destination till they were, every one of them, arrested and imprisoned. So far as I am aware, this was an instance of discipline and nonviolence for which there is no parallel in history. Without such restraint I see no hope of successful mass civil disobedience here.

We must dismiss the idea of overawing the Government by huge demonstrations every time someone is arrested. On the contrary we must treat arrest as the normal condition of the life of a non-co-operator. For we must seek arrest and imprisonment, as a soldier who goes to battle seeks death. We expect to bear down the opposition of the Government by courting and not by avoiding imprisonment, even though it be by showing our supposed readiness to be arrested and imprisoned en masse. Civil disobedience then emphatically means our desire to surrender to a single unarmed policeman. Our triumph consists in thousands being led to the prisons like lambs to the slaughter-house. If the lambs of the world had been willingly led, they would have long ago saved themselves from the butcher's knife. Our triumph consists again in being imprisoned for no wrong whatsoever. The greater our innocence, the greater our strength and the swifter our victory.

As it is, this Government is cowardly, we are afraid of imprisonment. The Government takes advantage of our fear of jails. If only our men and women welcome jails as health resorts, we will cease to worry about the dear ones put in jails which our countrymen in South Africa used to nickname His Majesty's Hotels.

We have too long been mentally disobedient to the laws of the State and have too often surreptitiously evaded them to be fit all of a sudden for civil disobedience. Disobedience to be civil has to be open and non-violent.

Complete civil disobedience is a state of peaceful rebellion—a refusal to obey every single State-made law. It is certainly more dangerous than an armed rebellion. For it can never be put down if the civil resisters are prepared to face extreme hardships. It is based upon an implicit belief in the absolute efficiency of innocent suffering. By noiselessly going to prison a civil resister ensures a calm atmosphere. The wrongdoer wearies of wrongdoing in the absence of resistance. All pleasure is lost when the victim betrays no resistance. A full grasp of the conditions of successful civil resistance is necessary at least on the part of the representatives of the people before we can launch out on an enterprise of such magnitude. The quickest remedies are always fraught with the greatest danger and require the utmost skill in handling them. It is my firm conviction that, if we bring about a successful boycott of foreign cloth, we shall have produced an atmosphere that would enable us to inaugurate civil disobedience on a scale that no Government can resist. I would therefore urge patience and determined concentration on swadeshi upon those who are impatient to embark on mass civil disobedience.[35]

LETTER TO LORD IRWIN

Satyagraha Ashram, Sabarmati
March 2, 1930

Dear Friend,

Before embarking on civil disobedience and taking the risk I have dreaded to take all these years, I would fain approach you and find a way out.

My personal faith is absolutely clear. I cannot intentionally hurt anything that lives, much less fellow human beings, even though they may do the greatest wrong to me and mine. Whilst, therefore, I hold the British rule to be a curse, I do not intend harm to a single Englishman or to any legitimate interest he may have in India.

I must not be misunderstood. Though I hold the British rule in India to be a curse, I do not, therefore, consider Englishmen in general to be worse than any other people on earth. I have the privilege of claiming many Englishmen as dearest friends. Indeed much that I have learnt of the evil of British rule is due to the writings of frank and courageous Englishmen who have not hesitated to tell the unpalatable truth about that rule.

And why do I regard the British rule as a curse?

It has impoverished the dumb millions by a system of progressive exploitation and by a ruinously expensive military and civil administration which the country can never afford.

It has reduced us politically to serfdom. It has sapped the foundations of our culture. And, by the policy of cruel disarmament, it has degraded us spiritually. Lacking the inward strength, we have been reduced, by all but universal disarmament, to a state bordering on cowardly helplessness. . . .

The terrific pressure of land revenue, which furnishes a large part of the total, must undergo considerable modification in an independent India. Even the much vaunted permanent settlement benefits the few rich zamindars [landlords], not the ryots [landless peasants]. The ryot has remained as helpless as ever. He is a mere tenant at will. Not only, then, has the land revenue to be considerably reduced, but the whole revenue system has to be so revised as to make the ryot's good its primary concern. But the British system seems to be designed to crush the very life out of him. Even the salt he must use to live is so taxed as to make the burden fall heaviest on him, if only because of the heartless impartiality of its incidence. The tax shows itself still more burdensome on the poor man when it is remembered that salt is the only thing he must eat more than the rich man both individually and collectively. The drink and drug revenue, too, is derived from the poor. It saps the foundations both of their health and morals. It is defended under the false plea of individual freedom, but, in reality, is maintained for its own sake. The ingenuity of the authors of the reforms of 1919 transferred this revenue to the so-called responsible part of dyarchy, so as to throw the burden of prohibition on it, thus, from the very beginning, rendering it powerless for good. If the unhappy minister wipes out this revenue he must starve education, since in the existing circumstances he has no new source of replacing that revenue. If the weight of taxation has crushed the poor from above, the destruction of the central supplementary industry, i.e., hand-spinning, has undermined their capacity for producing wealth. The tale of India's ruination is not complete without reference to the liabilities incurred in her name. Sufficient has been recently said about these in the public Press. It must be the duty of a free India to subject all the liabilities to the strictest investigation, and repudiate those that may be adjudged by an impartial tribunal to be unjust and unfair.

The inequities sampled above are maintained in order to carry on a foreign administration, demonstrably the most expensive in the world. Take your own salary. It is over Rs. 21,000 per month, besides many other indirect additions. The British Prime Minister gets £5,000 per year, i.e., over Rs. 5,400 per month at the present rate of exchange. You are getting over Rs. 700 per day against India's average income of less than annas 2 per day [= .125 rupee]. The Prime Minister gets Rs. 180 per day against Great Britain's average income of nearly Rs. 2 per day. Thus you are getting much over five thousand times India's average income. The British Prime Minister is getting only ninety times Britain's average income. On bended knees I ask you to ponder over this phenomenon. I have taken a personal illustration to drive home a painful truth. I have too great a regard for you as a man to wish to hurt your feelings. I know that you do not need the salary you get. Probably the whole of your salary goes for charity. But a system that provides for such an arrangement deserves to be summarily scrapped. What is true of the Viceregal salary is true generally of the whole administration.

A radical cutting down of the revenue, therefore, depends upon an equal radical reduction in the expenses of the administration. This means a transformation of the scheme of government. This transformation is impossible without independence. Hence, in my opinion, the spontaneous demonstration of 26th January, in which hundreds of thousands of villagers instinctively participated. To them independence means deliverance from the killing weight.

Not one of the great British political parties, it seems to me, is prepared to give up the Indian spoils to which Great Britain helps herself from day to day, often, in spite of the unanimous opposition of Indian opinion.

Nevertheless, if India is to live as a nation, if the slow death by starvation of her people is to stop, some remedy must be found for immediate relief. The proposed Conference is certainly not the remedy. It is not a matter of carrying conviction by argument. The matter resolves itself into one of matching forces. Conviction or no conviction, Great Britain would defend her Indian commerce and interests by all the forces at her command. India must consequently evolve force enough to free herself from that embrace of death.

It is common cause that, however disorganized and, for the time being, insignificant it may be, the party of violence is gaining ground and making itself felt. Its end is the same as mine. But I am convinced that it cannot bring the desired relief to the dumb millions. And the conviction is growing deeper and deeper in me that nothing but unadulterated non-violence can check the organized violence of the British Government. Many think that non-violence is not an active force. My experience, limited though it undoubtedly is, shows that non-violence can be an intensely active force. It is my purpose to set in motion that force as well against the organized violent force of the British rule as [against] the unorganized violent force of the growing party of violence. To sit still would be to give rein to both the forces above mentioned. Having an unquestioning and immovable faith in the efficacy of non-violence as I know it, it would be sinful on my part to wait any longer.

This non-violence will be expressed through civil disobedience, for the moment confined to the inmates of the Satyagraha Ashram, but ultimately designed to cover all those who choose to join the movement with its obvious limitations.

I know that in embarking on non-violence I shall be running what might fairly be termed a mad risk. But the victories of truth have never been won without risks, often of the gravest character. Conversion of a nation that has consciously or unconsciously preyed upon another, far more numerous, far more ancient and no less cultured than itself, is worth any amount of risk.

I have deliberately used the word "conversion." For my ambition is no less than to convert the British people through non-violence, and thus make them see the wrongs they have done to India. I do not seek to harm your people. I want to serve them even as I want to serve my own. I believe that I have always served them. I served them up to 1919 blindly. But when my eyes were opened and I conceived non-co-operation, the object still was to serve them. I employed the same weapon that I have in all humility successfully used against the dearest members of my family. If I have equal love for your people with mine it will not long remain hidden. It will be acknowledged by them even as the members of my family acknowledged it after they had tried me for several years. If the people join me as I expect they will, the sufferings they will undergo, unless the British nation sooner retraces its steps, will be enough to melt the stoniest hearts.

The plan through civil disobedience will be to combat such evils as I have sampled out. If we want to sever the British connection it is because of such evils. When they are removed the path becomes easy. Then the way to friendly negotiation will be open. If the British commerce with India is purified of greed, you will have no difficulty in recognizing our independence. I respectfully invite you then to pave the way for immediate removal of those evils, and thus open a way for a real conference between equals, interested only in promoting the common good of mankind through voluntary fellowship and in arranging terms of mutual help and commerce equally suited to both. You have unnecessarily laid stress upon the communal problems that unhappily affect this land. Important though they undoubtedly are for the consideration of any scheme of government, they have little bearing on the greater problems which are above communities and which affect them all equally. But if you cannot see your way to deal with these evils and my letter makes no appeal to your heart, on the 11th day of this month,* I shall proceed with such co-workers of the Ashram as I can take, to disregard the provisions of the salt laws. I regard this tax to be the most iniquitous of all from the poor man's standpoint. As the independence movement is essentially for the poorest in the land the beginning will be made with this evil. The wonder is that we have submitted to the cruel monopoly for so long. It is, I know, open to you to frustrate my design by arresting me. I hope that there will be tens of thousands ready, in a disciplined manner, to take up the work after me, and, in the act of disobeying the Salt Act to lay themselves open to the penalties of a law that should never have disfigured the Statute-book.

*The march, however, started on March 12.

I have no desire to cause you unnecessary embarrassment, or any at all, so far as I can help. If you think that there is any substance in my letter, and if you will care to discuss matters with me, and if to that end you would like me to postpone publication of this letter, I shall gladly refrain on receipt of a telegram to that effect soon after this reaches you.* You will, however, do me the favor not to deflect me from my course unless you can see your way to conform to the substance of this letter.

This letter is not in any way intended as a threat but it is a simple and sacred duty peremptory on a civil resister. Therefore I am having it specially delivered by a young English friend who believes in the Indian cause and is a full believer in non-violence and whom Providence seems to have sent to me, as it were, for the very purpose.†

I remain,
Your sincere friend,
M. K. Gandhi[36]

DUTY OF DISLOYALTY

There is no halfway house between active loyalty and active disloyalty. There is much truth in the late Justice Stephen's remark that a man to prove himself not guilty of disaffection must prove himself to be actively affectionate. In these days of democracy there is no such thing as active loyalty to a person. You are therefore loyal or disloyal to institutions. When therefore you are disloyal you seek not to destroy persons by institutions. The present State is an institution which, if one knows it, can never evoke loyalty. It is corrupt. Many of its laws governing the conduct of persons are positively inhuman. Their administration is worse. Often the will of one person is the law. It may safely be said that there are as many rulers as there are districts in this country. These, called Collectors, combine in their own persons the executive as well as the judicial functions. Though their acts are supposed to be governed by laws in themselves highly defective,

---

*The Viceroy's reply was simply an expression of regret that Gandhi should be "contemplating a course of action which is clearly bound to involve violation of the law and danger to the public peace."

†Reginald Reynolds, who took the letter to the Viceroy, observes in *To Live in Mankind*: "Before I went Gandhi insisted I should read the letter carefully, as he did not wish me to associate myself with it unless I was in complete agreement with its contents. My taking of this letter was, in fact, intended to be symbolic of the fact that this was not merely a struggle between the Indians and the British."

these rulers are often capricious and regulated by nothing but their own whims and fancies. They represent not the interests of the people but those of their foreign masters or principals. These (nearly three hundred) men form an almost secret corporation, the most powerful in the world. They are required to find a fixed minimum of revenue, they have therefore often been found to be most unscrupulous in their dealings with the people. This system of government is confessedly based upon a merciless exploitation of unnumbered millions of the inhabitants of India. From the village Headmen to their personal assistants these satraps have created a class of subordinates who, whilst they cringe before their foreign masters, in their constant dealings with the people act so irresponsibly and so harshly as to demoralize them and by a system of terrorism render them incapable of resisting corruption. It is then the duty of those who have realized the awful evil of the system of Indian Government to be disloyal to it and actively and openly to preach disloyalty. Indeed, loyalty to a State so corrupt is a sin, disloyalty a virtue.

The spectacle of three hundred million people being cowed down by living in the dread of three hundred men is demoralizing alike for the despots as for the victims. It is the duty of those who have realized the evil nature of the system however attractive some of its feature may, torn from their context, appear to be, to destroy it without delay. It is their clear duty to run any risk to achieve the end.

But it must be equally clear that it would be cowardly for three hundred million people to seek to destroy the three hundred authors or administrators of the system. It is a sign of gross ignorance to devise means of destroying these administrators or their hirelings. Moreover, they are but creatures of circumstances. The purest man entering the system will be affected by it and will be instrumental in propagating the evil. The remedy therefore naturally is not being enraged against the administrators and therefore hurting them, but to non-co-operate with the system by withdrawing all the voluntary assistance possible and refusing all its so-called benefits. A little reflection will show that civil disobedience is a necessary part of non-co-operation. You assist an administration most effectively by obeying its orders and decrees. An evil administration never deserves such allegiance. Allegiance to it means partaking of the evil. A good man will therefore resist an evil system or administration with his whole soul. Disobedience of the law of an evil State is therefore a duty. Violent disobedience deals with men who can be replaced. It leaves the evil itself untouched and often accentuates it. Non-violent, i.e., civil, disobedience is the only and the most successful remedy and is obligatory upon him who would dissociate himself from evil.

There is danger in civil disobedience only because it is still only a partially tried remedy and has always to be tried in an atmosphere surcharged with violence. For when tyranny is rampant much rage is generated among victims. It remains latent because of their weakness and bursts in all its fury on the slightest pretext. Civil disobedience is a sovereign method of transmuting this undisciplined life-destroying latent energy into disciplined life-saving energy whose use ensures absolute success. The attendant risk is nothing compared to the result promised. When the world has become familiar with its use and when it has had a series of demonstrations of its successful working, there will be less risk in civil disobedience than there is in aviation, in spite of that science having reached a high stage of development.[37]

SOME RULES OF SATYAGRAHA

Satyagraha literally means insistence on truth. This insistence arms the votary with matchless power. This power or force is connected by the word satyagraha. Satyagraha, to be genuine, may be offered against parents, against one's wife or one's children, against rulers, against fellow-citizens, even against the whole world.

Such a universal force necessarily makes no distinction between kinsmen and strangers, young and old, man and woman, friend and foe. The force to be so applied can never be physical. There is in it no room for violence. The only force of universal application can, therefore, be that of ahimsa or love. In other words it is soul force.

Love does not burn others, it burns itself. Therefore, a satyagrahi, i.e., a civil resister will joyfully suffer even unto death.

It follows, therefore, that a civil resister, whilst he will strain every nerve to compass the end of the existing rule, will do no intentional injury in thought, word or deed to the person of a single Englishman. This necessarily brief explanation of satyagraha will perhaps enable the reader to understand and appreciate the following rules:

As an Individual

1. A satyagrahi, i.e., a civil resister will harbour no anger.
2. He will suffer the anger of the opponent.
3. In so doing he will put up with assaults from the opponent, never retaliate; but he will not submit, out of fear of punishment or the like, to any order given in anger.
4. When any person in authority seeks to arrest a civil resister, he will voluntarily submit to the arrest, and he will not resist the

attachment or removal of his own property, if any, when it is sought to be confiscated by authorities.

5. If a civil resister has any property in his possession as a trustee, he will refuse to surrender it, even though in defending it he might lose his life. He will, however, never retaliate.
6. Non-retaliation excludes swearing and cursing.
7. Therefore a civil resister will never insult his opponent, and therefore also not take part in many of the newly coined cries which are contrary to the spirit of ahimsa.
8. A civil resister will not salute the Union Jack, nor will he insult it or officials, English or Indian.
9. In the course of the struggle if anyone insults an official or commits an assault upon him, a civil resister will protect such official or officials from the insult or attack even at the risk of his life.

As a Prisoner

10. As a prisoner, a civil resister will behave courteously towards prison officials, and will observe all such discipline of the prison as is not contrary to self-respect; as for instance, whilst he will salaam officials in the usual manner, he will not perform any humiliating gyrations and [will] refuse to shout "Victory to Sarkar" [Government] or the like. He will take cleanly cooked and cleanly served food, which is not contrary to his religion, and will refuse to take food insultingly served or served in unclean vessels.
11. A civil resister will make no distinction between an ordinary prisoner and himself, will in no way regard himself as superior to the rest, nor will he ask for any conveniences that may not be necessary for keeping his body in good health and condition. He is entitled to ask for such conveniences as may be required for his physical or spiritual well-being.
12. A civil resister may not fast for want of conveniences whose deprivation does not involve any injury to one's self-respect.

As a Unit

13. A civil resister will joyfully obey all the orders issued by the leader of the corps, whether they please him or not.
14. He will carry out orders in the first instance even though they appear to him insulting, inimical or foolish, and then appeal to higher authority. He is free before joining to determine the fitness of the corps to satisfy him, but after he has joined it, it becomes a duty to submit to its discipline irksome or otherwise. If the sum total of the

energy of the corps appears to a member to be improper or immoral, he has a right to sever his connection, but being with it, he has no right to commit a breach of its discipline.

15. No civil resister is to expect maintenance for his dependents. It would be an accident if any such provision is made. A civil resister entrusts his dependents to the care of God. Even in ordinary warfare wherein hundreds of thousands give themselves up to it, they are able to make no previous provision. How much more, then should be the case in satyagraha? It is the universal experience that in such times hardly anybody is left to starve.

In Communal Fights

16. No civil resister will intentionally become a cause of communal [religious] quarrels.

17. In the event of any such outbreak, he will not take sides, but he will assist only that party which is demonstrably in the right. Being a Hindu he will be generous towards Mussalmans and others, and will sacrifice himself in the attempt to save non-Hindus from a Hindu attack. And if the attack is from the other side, he will not participate in any retaliation but will give his life in protecting Hindus.

18. He will, to the best of his ability, avoid every occasion that may give rise to communal quarrels.

19. If there is a procession of satyagrahis they will do nothing that would wound the religious susceptibilities of any community, and they will not take part in any other processions that are likely to wound such susceptibilities.[38]

"RENDER UNTO CAESAR"

An unknown English friend has thought it worth while cabling to me that in launching upon civil disobedience I am going against the teaching of Jesus: "Render unto Caesar that which is Caesar's." Another, an Indian Christian, writes from the Punjab somewhat in the same fashion and, forsaking charity, pours abuse upon my devoted head for my action. He says further that whereas he considered me to be a good man formerly, he is now utterly undeceived. I can assure this friend that civil disobedience is no new thing with me. I began to preach and practice it in 1906. His regard for me therefore was evidently from ignorance, if his present dislike of me is wise. But I have learnt from the New Testament, as also from other sources, that if one wishes to walk in the fear of God, one should be indifferent about popular praise or blame.

Now for the question. As I hold my conduct to be in utter agreement
with universal religion and as I hold the New Testament teaching in great
esteem, I should not like it to be justly said of me that I was going against
the teaching of Jesus. "Render unto Caesar" was quoted against me before
too. I have not read into the celebrated verse the meaning that my critics
have sought to put into it. Jesus evaded the direct question put to him because it was a trap. He was in no way bound to answer it. He therefore
asked to see the coin for taxes. And then said with withering scorn, "How
can you who traffic in Caesar's coins and thus receive what to you are benefits of Caesar's rule refuse to pay taxes?" Jesus's whole preaching and
practice point unmistakably to non-co-operation, which necessarily includes non-payment of taxes. Jesus never recognized man's authority as
against God's. He who disregarded the whole host of priesthood, which
was in those days superior to kinghood, would not have hesitated to defy
the might of emperors had he found it necessary. And did he not treat
with supreme disdain the whole of the farcical trial through which he was
made to pass?[39]

------

*The march and the fast were the two most dramatically successful branches
in Gandhi's tree of* satyagraha. *Although he gave primacy to his "constructive
program" of social reforms to attain* swaraj, *history will remember Gandhi
for his salt march of 1930 and then for his heroic fasts to contain the violence
of India's civil war in 1947–48.*

*The ongoing conflict between India's Hindu majority and Muslim minority
occurred mainly in the northern area of the country, where millions had
converted to Islam. This conflict was called "communal" violence, and
Gandhi's response to the Hindu-Muslim problem is examined at length in
Part II, as one of the major social reforms in his constructive program. The
violence had erupted periodically during the nationalist movement but it
reached an unprecedented level in August 1946, when the civil war began in
Calcutta. India was now only a year away from its independence. The
Muslims, led by M. A. Jinnah and the Muslim League, demanded a separate
state of Pakistan, a land of Islam, located in the northwestern and north-
eastern Muslim-majority regions of India. The creation of Pakistan thus
caused the "partition" of India, an event which Gandhi opposed as a "vivi-
section" of the subcontinent. Although he failed when Pakistan became a
reality, he proved the efficacy of nonviolence even in the midst of civil war.*

*A correspondent whom Gandhi quotes in the first article of this section
addresses the question that immediately concerned Gandhi when large-scale
communal violence struck: "How can non-violence be efficacious during*

riots?" Gandhi's response is based on a philosophy that begins with the
acceptance of responsibility for the so-called criminal elements that were
often blamed for violence. After this comes a series of articles on his theory
of fasting.

A friend writes:

How can non-violence be efficacious during riots? By self-immolation we can
influence only those with whom we have already established living contacts.
But the hooligans who perpetrate violence during riots are, as a rule, hirelings
imported from outside. How can they have any scruples about hurting those
whom they have never known before and for whom they can have no regard or
consideration?

The question deserves careful consideration. The friend who has put
it is a valiant worker who nearly lost his life in trying to do his duty during
a riot.

I have often written on this question before. The pity of it is that Congressmen have never seriously thought over the question of finding a non-
violent way of quelling riots. Their non-violence was restricted to the sole
purpose of offering civil resistance to the authorities. In my opinion the
non-violence that goes so far and no further scarcely deserves the name
"ahimsa." You may, if you like, call it unarmed resistance. So far as it is
a device for embarrassing the Government it is a species of himsa [vio-
lence]. To quell riots non-violently, there must be true ahimsa in one's
heart, an ahimsa that takes even the erring hooligan in its warm embrace.
Such an attitude has to be cultivated. It can only come as a prolonged and
patient effort which must be made during peaceful times. The would-be
members of a peace brigade should come into close touch and cultivate
acquaintance with the so-called goonda [hooligan or thug] element in his
vicinity. He should know all and be known to all and win the hearts of
all by his living and selfless service. No section should be regarded as
too contemptible or mean to mix with. Goondas do not drop from the sky,
nor do they spring from the earth like evil spirits. They are the product of
social disorganization, and society is therefore responsible for their exis
tence. In other words, they should be looked upon as a symptom of corruption in our body politic. To remove the disease we must first discover
the underlying cause. To find the remedy will then be a comparatively
easy task. So far we have not even attempted a proper beginning. But it is
never too late to mend. It is enough that we are at last alive to the necessity
of it. We have now to follow it up with prompt action. Let everyone who is

interested make a prompt beginning in his own neighborhood. The difficulty mentioned by my correspondent will automatically resolve itself if we proceed with our effort in the right spirit.[40]

Can you fast against the goondas? [question asked Gandhi on the eve of the Calcutta fast]

[He replied:] The conflagration has been caused not by the goondas but by those who have become goondas. It is we who make goondas. Without our sympathy and passive support, the goondas would have no legs to stand upon. I want to touch the hearts of those who are behind the goondas.

But must you launch your fast at this stage? Why not wait and watch a little?

It would be too late afterwards. The minority Muslims cannot be left in a perilous state. My fast has to be preventive if it is to be any good. I know I shall be able to tackle the Punjab too if I can control Calcutta. But if I falter now, the conflagration may spread.[41]

If and when the call comes to fast unto death, I will do so irrespective of others joining or not. Fasting unto death is the last and the most potent weapon in the armory of satyagraha. It is a sacred thing. But it must be accepted with all its implications. It is not the fast itself but what it implies that matters. Have not even hypocrites been known to make a pretense of fasting? Such fasts are a plague and a nuisance. They do not count. If I fast and you send a hundred or even ten men who would undertake it with a pure heart, I shall be happy. But such a fast should be undertaken inside the prison.[42]

I have had the temerity to claim that fasting is an infallible weapon in the armory of satyagraha. I have used it myself, being the author of Satyagraha. . . .

One general principle, however, I would like to enunciate. A satyagrahi should fast only as a last resort when all other avenues of redress have been explored and have failed. There is no room for imitation in fasts. He who has no inner strength should not dream of it, and never with attachment to success. But, if a satyagrahi once undertakes a fast from conviction, he must stick to his resolve whether there is a chance of his action bearing fruit or not. This does not mean that fasting cannot bear fruit. He who fasts in the expectation of fruit generally fails. And even if he does not seemingly fail, he loses all the inner joy which a true fast holds.

Whether one should take fruit-juices or not depends on one's physical powers of endurance. But no more fruit-juice than is absolutely necessary for the body should be taken. He probably has the greatest inner strength who takes only water.

It is wrong to fast for selfish ends, e.g., for increase in one's own salary. Under certain circumstances it is permissible to fast for an increase in wages on behalf of one's group. Ridiculous fasts spread like plague and are harmful. But when fasting becomes a duty, it cannot be given up. Therefore I do fast when I consider it to be necessary and cannot abstain from it on any score. What I do myself I cannot prevent others from doing under similar circumstances. It is common knowledge that the best of good things are often abused. We see this happening every day.[43]

Q. Are not all fasts violent? Do I not coerce a friend when I try to prevent him, by means of my fast, from doing a wrong act?

A. Fasts undertaken according to the rules governing them are truly non-violent. There is no room there for coercion. If a friend of mine is going astray, and if I impose suffering on myself by fasting in order to awaken his better instincts, it can be only out of love. If the friend from whom I fast has no love in him, he will not respond. If he has it and responds, it is all to the good. This is how I would analyze his act: He valued his love for me more than his bad ways. There is a possible risk, I admit, namely that as soon as the effect of the fast is over he would be tempted to go back to his old ways. But then I can fast again. Ultimately the increasing influence of my love will either convert the friend to the extent of weaning him completely from his evil ways, or repeated fasts may lose their novelty, blunt his mind, and make it impervious to my fasting. It is my conviction that a fast undertaken out of genuine love cannot have such an untoward result. But because such a result is not impossible we cannot afford to disregard this pure instrument of moral reform. The risk, however, makes it clear that he who fasts should be properly qualified, and that it should not be lightly undertaken.[44]

FASTING IN NON-VIOLENT ACTION

If the struggle which we are seeking to avoid with all our might has to come,* and if it is to remain non-violent as it must in order to succeed, fasting is likely to play an important part in it. It has its place in the tussle with authority and with our own people in the event of wanton acts of violence and obstinate riots for instance.

*This anticipates the "Quit India" campaign, the last large-scale civil disobedience action against the British of 1942–44, during which Gandhi fasted while in prison.

There is a natural prejudice against it as part of a political struggle. It has a recognized place in religious practice. But it is considered a vulgar interpolation in politics by the ordinary politician though it has always been resorted to by prisoners in a haphazard way with more or less success. By fasting, however, they have always succeeded in drawing public attention and disturbing peace of jail authorities.

My own fasts have always, as I hold, been strictly according to the law of satyagraha. . . .

Fasting . . . is the greatest force because of the limitless scope it affords for self-suffering without causing or intending any physical or material injury to the wrongdoer. The object always is to evoke the best in him. Self-suffering is an appeal to his better nature, as retaliation is to his baser. Fasting under proper circumstances is such an appeal par excellence. If the politician does not perceive its propriety in political matters, it is because it is a novel use of this very fine weapon.

To practice non-violence in mundane matters is to know its true value. It is to bring heaven upon earth. There is no such thing as the other world. All worlds are one. There is no "here" and no "there." As Jeans has demonstrated, the whole universe including the most distant stars, invisible even through the most powerful telescope in the world, is compressed in an atom. I hold it therefore to be wrong to limit the use of non-violence to cave-dwellers and for acquiring merit for a favored position in the other world. All virtue ceases to have use if it serves no purpose in every walk of life. I would therefore plead with the purely political-minded people to study non-violence and fasting as its extreme manifestation with sympathy and understanding.[45]

WAS IT COERCIVE?

. . . Fasting has been for years past an integral part of my life and I may have to resume it whether outside or inside prison walls. I cannot, therefore, write too often on the science of fasting, if I may use the sacred word "science" in connection with my fasts. . . .

. . . I do admit that my fast of September [1932] did unfortunately coerce some people into action which they would not have endorsed without my fast. I do admit also that my last fast coerced the Government into releasing me. I admit, too, that such coercion can and does sometimes lead to insincere conduct. . . .

These admissions do not cut at the very root of fasts. They only show that there is great need for caution and that special qualifications are necessary for those who would resort to fasting as a method of reform or securing justice. . . .

. . . My definite opinion is that the general result of my numerous fasts was without doubt beneficial. They invariably quickened the conscience of the people interested in and sought to be influenced by those fasts. I am not aware of any injustice having been perpetrated through those fasts. . . . In no case was there any idea of exercising coercion on anyone. Indeed, I think that the word coercion would be a misnomer for the influence that was exerted by the fasts under criticism. Coercion means some harmful force used against a person who is expected to do something desired by the user of the force. In the fasts in question, the force used was against myself. Surely, force of self-suffering cannot be put in the same category as the force of suffering caused to the party sought to be influenced. If I fast in order to awaken the conscience of an erring friend whose error is beyond question, I am not coercing him in the ordinary sense of the word. . . .

Of course, it is not to be denied that fasts can be really coercive. Such are fasts to attain a selfish object. A fast undertaken to wring money from a person or for fulfilling some such personal end would amount to the exercise of coercion or undue influence. I would unhesitatingly advocate resistance of such undue influence. I have myself successfully resisted it in the fasts that have been undertaken or threatened against me. And if it is argued that the dividing line between a selfish and an unselfish end is often very thin, I would urge that a person who regards the end of a fast to be selfish or otherwise base should resolutely refuse to yield to it, even though the refusal may result in the death of the fasting person. If people will cultivate the habit of disregarding fasts which in their opinion are taken for unworthy ends, such fasts will be robbed of the taint of coercion and undue influence. Like all human institutions, fasting can be both legitimately and illegitimately used. But as a great weapon in the armory of satyagraha, it cannot be given up because of its possible abuse. Satyagraha has been designed as an effective substitute for violence. This use is in its infancy and, therefore, not yet perfected. But as the author of modern satyagraha I cannot give up any of its manifold uses without forfeiting my claim to handle it in the spirit of a humble seeker.[46]

Fasting in satyagraha has well-defined limits. You cannot fast against a tyrant. . . . Fasting can only be resorted to against a lover, not to extort rights but to reform him, as when a son fasts for a parent who drinks. My fast at Bombay, and then at Bardoli, was of that character. I fasted to reform those who loved me. But I will not fast to reform, say, General

Dyer who not only does not love me, but who regards himself as my
enemy.[47]

The words 'tyrant' and 'lover' have also a general application. The one
who does an injustice is styled 'tyrant.' The one who is in sympathy with
you is the 'lover.' . . . There are two conditions attached to a satyagrahi
fast. It should be against the lover and for his reform, not for extorting
rights from him. . . . I can fast against my father to cure him of a vice, but
I may not in order to get from him an inheritance. The beggars of India
who sometimes fast against those who do not satisfy them are no more
satyagrahis than children who fast against a parent for a fine dress.[48]

The first part of the readings on the theory and practice of satyagraha
*suggests that a study and an appreciation of Gandhi's significance begins with
an understanding of his idea of power. As indicated in Part II,* satyagraha *is
consistently related to his idea of* swaraj *or freedom, and the concepts should
be examined together. Gandhi's originality as a political thinker lies here; its
revolutionary spirit was emphasized by Jawaharlal Nehru:*

> *It is not surprising that this astonishingly vital man, full of self-confidence and an
> unusual kind of power, standing for equality and freedom for each individual, but
> measuring all this in terms of the poorest, fascinated the masses of India and
> attracted them like a magnet. He seemed to them to link up the past with the future
> and to make the dismal present appear just as a steppingstone to that future of life
> and hope. And not the masses only, but intellectuals and others also, though their
> minds were often troubled and confused and the change-over for them from the
> habits of lifetimes was more difficult. Thus he effected a vast psychological revo-
> lution not only among those who followed his lead but also among his opponents
> and those many neutrals who could not make up their minds what to think and
> what to do.[49]*

*The final comment by Gandhi in this section illustrates once again his
awareness of what we have come to know as "people power," or the force that
"empowers the powerless," phrases that have become common coin, especially
since the fall of authoritarian governments in the Philippines, Eastern Europe,
and South Africa. Gandhi would have understood these revolutionary
changes, just as we can understand them better in light of his achievement.*

We have long been accustomed to think that power comes only through
Legislative Assemblies. I have regarded this belief as a grave error brought
about by inertia or hypnotism. A superficial study of British history has
made us think that all power percolates to the people from parliaments.

The truth is that power resides in the people and it is entrusted for the time being to those whom they may choose as their representatives. Parliaments have no power or even existence independently of the people. It has been my effort for the last twenty-one years to convince the people of this simple truth. Civil disobedience is the storehouse of power. Imagine a whole people unwilling to conform to the laws of the legislature, and prepared to suffer the consequences of non-compliance. They will bring the whole legislative and executive machinery to a standstill. The police and the military are of use to coerce minorities however powerful they may be. But no police or military coercion can bend the resolute will of a people who are out for suffering to the uttermost.[50]

To me political power is not an end but one of the means of enabling people to better their condition in every department of life. Political power means capacity to regulate national life through national representatives. If national life becomes so perfect as to become self-regulated, no representation is necessary. There is then a state of enlightened anarchy. In such a state everyone is his own ruler. He rules himself in such a manner that he is never a hindrance to his neighbor. In the ideal state therefore there is no political power because there is no State. But the ideal is never fully realized in life. Hence the classical statement of Thoreau that the Government is best which governs the least.[51]

Notes to Part I

1. *CWMG* 25: 563. January 8, 1925.
2. *CWMG* 54: 416–17. April 15, 1933.
3. *CWMG* 33: 245–47. April 21, 1927.
4. *CWMG* 22: 416–21. February 16, 1922.
5. *CWMG* 15: 244. April 21, 1919.
6. *CWMG* 21: 472–75. November 20, 1921.
7. *CWMG* 21: 457. November 17, 1921.
8. *CWMG* 46: 202. May 28, 1931.
9. Ibid., 359. June 11, 1931.
10. *CWMG* 39: 61. April 18, 1926.
11. Ibid., 114.
12. *CWMG* 10: 306–7. August 15, 1910.
13. *CWMG* 10: 1–2, 4. November 18, 1909.
14. *CWMG* 13: 294–95. October 1916.
15. *CWMG* 23: 24–25, 27. March 9, 1922.
16. *CWMG* 25: 423–24. December 11, 1924.
17. *CWMG* 27: 131–35. May 21, 1925.
18. *CWMG* 44: 56–59. July 28, 1930.
19. *CWMG* 21: 550–52. December 8, 1921.
20. *CWMG* 22: 43–46. December 18, 1921.
21. *CWMG* 19: 220–21. January 12, 1921.
22. *CWMG* 21: 451. November 17, 1921.
23. *CWMG* 19: 466–67. March 23, 1921.
24. *CWMG* 13: 520–26. September 2, 1917.
25. *CWMG* 14: 63–65. November 3, 1917.
26. *CWMG* 18: 92–93. July 28, 1920.
27. *CWMG* 21: 313–14. October 20, 1921.
28. *CWMG* 18: 230–31. September 5, 1920.
29. *CWMG* 16: 368–70, 378–83, 387–90, 409.
30. *CWMG* 18: 146–53. August 12, 1920.
31. Ibid., 125–29. August 15, 1920.
32. Dalton, *Mahatma Gandhi*, 91, 215.
33. *CWMG* 43: 180–81. April 5, 1930.

34. *Time*, January 5, 1931, 14–15.
35. *CWMG* 20: 464–66. August 4, 1921.
36. *CWMG* 43: 2–8. March 2, 1930.
37. Ibid., 132–34. March 27, 1930.
38. *CWMG* 42: 491–93. February 27, 1930.
39. *CWMG* 43: 131–32. March 27, 1930.
40. *CWMG* 72: 455-56. September 15, 1940.
41. *CWMG* 89: 132-33. September 1, 1947.
42. *CWMG* 85: 147. August 10, 1946.
43. *CWMG* 83: 401. April 13, 1946.
44. *CWMG* 72: 458. September 10, 1940.
45. *CWMG* 76: 317–19. July 20, 1942.
46. *CWMG* 55: 411–13. September 9, 1933.
47. *CWMG* 23: 420. April 12, 1924.
48. Ibid., 517. May 1, 1924.
49. Nehru, *Discovery of India*, 385.
50. *CWMG* 75: 148. December 13, 1941.
51. *CWMG* 47: 91. July 2, 1931.

Part II

SWARAJ:
GANDHI'S IDEA
OF FREEDOM

INTRODUCTION

When Gandhi wrote in 1909 that India's freedom struggle had misunderstood the "real significance" of swaraj *by equating it with independence, and that "my life henceforth is dedicated" to realizing its true meaning,[1] it was a signal that he would build around this word* swaraj *a cluster of ideas. At the center of this cluster came the tight conceptual relationship of* swaraj *to* satyagraha, *arguing that the only way to real freedom was through nonviolent action. If* satyagraha *had, as he said, "many branches," so did* swaraj. *After Gandhi assumed leadership of the nationalist movement, he tried to spell out for India the many meanings of freedom.*

Gandhi's theory must be considered in the historical context of a colonized country, and it gains significance from the way that it interprets freedom from colonialism. Ashis Nandy, an astute analyst of Indian culture, observed that "colonialism is first of all a matter of consciousness and needs to be defeated ultimately in the minds of men." This meant that in India's struggle, "the liberation ultimately had to begin from the colonized and end with the colonizers. As Gandhi was to so clearly formulate through his own life, freedom is indivisible, not only in the popular sense that the oppressed of the world are one but also in the unpopular sense that the oppressor too is caught in the culture of oppression."[2] This was a realization that both Gandhi and Nehru gained after the Amritsar massacre: if India and Britain alike were caught in the lethal grip of a colonial mentality, then swaraj *could mean a mutual liberation from a domination-submission symbiosis. When Gandhi moved from a narrow separatism to inclusivism after 1919, it was with this larger understanding of how a common sense of humanity must overcome "the culture of oppression" that afflicted everyone in India.*

Just as Gandhi argued in the context of his theory of satyagraha *that power was of two kinds, violent and nonviolent, so he believed that in his interpretation of* swaraj *freedom had both internal and external aspects. He sounded this key note of his philosophy on many occasions in these terms: "The outward freedom therefore that we shall attain will only be in exact proportion to the inward freedom to which we may have grown at a given* moment. *And if this is the correct view of freedom, our chief energy must be concentrated upon achieving reform from within.*[3] *National independence or "outward" freedom is just one part of* swaraj, *only a "means of measuring the freedom of the self within." The right aim, he says, of those "who wish to attain true freedom" should be "an improvement in the self."*[4] *This relates to Ashis Nandy's point that liberation ultimately demanded a contest of consciousness waged within that "had to begin from the colonized." Gandhi was that rare political leader who demanded of his followers self-examination and "reform from within."*

This idea of "inward freedom" implies that swaraj *requires a personal journey or search for self-knowledge that liberates one from the sort of fear and insecurity that fuels both a desire to dominate or to be dominated. It was the willingness of Indians to cooperate with the British raj out of fear that troubled Gandhi. "Inward freedom" implies personal liberation from such fear. Gandhi recognized that this freedom was not easily gained in any society plagued by gross inequality and exploitation, but he insisted that Indians must be held responsible for collaborating with the government. "The pilgrimage to Swaraj," he said, "is a painful climb."*[5] *His own life can be seen as an arduous journey. As such, it can be compared with the lives of others who have suffered from racism and whose response might be viewed as a personal struggle for freedom from fear and domination. The comparison with Malcolm X suggested in the Introduction is worthwhile because their two extraordinary autobiographies portray similar paths to self-realization. Each finds a passage from emulation through separatism to inclusivity that finally transcends racial antinomies. Gandhi and Malcolm assume almost as an obligation the personal quest that lies at the heart of* swaraj.

This selection from Gandhi's voluminous writings on swaraj *begins with the familiar theme that the goal of* swaraj *"is infinitely greater than and includes independence" because it means not merely "the change of government" from British to Indian rule but "a real change of heart on the part of the people." Only this can produce necessary social reforms such as abolition of untouchability, the formation of Hindu–Muslim unity, and sexual and economic equality. All these elements of* swaraj *can be attained solely through* satyagraha: *"India's freedom," he concludes, "lies only through non-violence and no other method."*

INDEPENDENCE V. SWARAJ

I submit that swaraj is an all-satisfying goal for all time. . . . It is infinitely greater than and includes independence. It is a vital word. It has been sanctified by the noble sacrifices of thousands of Indians. It is a word

which, if it has not penetrated the remotest corner of India, has at least got
the largest currency of any similar word. It is a sacrilege to displace that
word by a foreign importation of doubtful value. . . .

I long for freedom from the English yoke. I would pay any price for it. I
would accept chaos in exchange for it. For the English peace is the peace
of the grave. Anything would be better than this living death of a whole
people. This Satanic rule has well-nigh ruined this fair land materially,
morally and spiritually. I daily see its law-courts denying justice and mur-
dering truth. . . . In order to protect its immoral commerce, this rule regards no means too mean, and in order to keep three hundred millions
under the heels of a hundred thousand, it carries a military expenditure
which is keeping millions in a state of semi-starvation and polluting thousands of mouths with intoxicating liquor.

But my creed is non-violence under all circumstances. My method
is conversion, not coercion; it is self-suffering, not the suffering of the
tyrant. I know that method to be infallible. I know that a whole people can
adopt it without accepting it as its creed and without understanding its
philosophy. People generally do not understand the philosophy of all their
acts. My ambition is much higher than independence. Through the deliverance of India, I seek to deliver the so-called weaker races of the earth
from the crushing heels of Western exploitation in which England is the
greatest partner. If India converts, as it can convert, Englishmen, it can
become the predominant partner in a world commonwealth of which
England can have the privilege of becoming a partner if she chooses. India
has the right, if she only knew, of becoming the predominant partner by
reason of her numbers, geographical position and culture inherited for
ages. This is big talk, I know. For a fallen India to aspire to move the world
and protect weaker races is seemingly an impertinence. But in explaining
my strong opposition to this cry for independence, I can no longer hide
the light under a bushel. Mine is an ambition worth living for and worth
dying for. In no case do I want to reconcile myself to a state lower than the
best for fear of consequences. It is, therefore, not out of expedience that I
oppose independence as my goal. I want India to come to her own and that
state cannot be better defined by any single word than "swaraj." Its content will vary with the action that the nation is able to put forth at a given
moment. India's coming to her own will mean every nation doing likewise.[6]

Swaraj does consist in the change of government and its real control by
the people, but that would be merely the form. The substance that I am
hankering after is a definite acceptance of the means and therefore a real
change of heart on the part of the people. I am certain that it does not require ages for Hindus to discard the error of untouchability, for Hindus

and Mussulmans to shed enmity and accept heart-friendship as an eternal factor of national life, for all to adopt the charkha [the spinning wheel as a symbol of identification with India's poor] as the only universal means of attaining India's economic salvation and finally for all to believe that India's freedom lies only through non-violence and no other method. Definite, intelligent and free adoption by the nation of this program I hold as the attainment of the substance. The symbol, the transfer of power, is sure to follow, even as the seed truly laid must develop into a tree.[7]

But after all, self-government depends entirely upon our own internal strength, upon our ability to fight against the heaviest odds. Indeed, self-government which does not require that continuous striving to attain it and to sustain it is not worth the name. I have therefore endeavored to show both in word and in deed that political self-government, that is, self-government for a large number of men and women, is no better than individual self-government, and therefore it is to be attained by precisely the same means that are required for individual self-government or self-rule, and so as you know also, I have striven in India to place this ideal before the people, in season and out of season, very often much to the disgust of those who are merely politically minded.[8]

Swaraj is not going to descend on us from the heavens. It will not be received as a gift from the British Empire either. It can only be the reward of our own efforts. The very word swaraj means effort by the nation. . . . No one will be able to stand in our way when we have developed the strength to win swaraj. Everyone's freedom is within his own grasp.

There are two alternatives before us. The one is that of violence, the other of non-violence; the one of physical strength, the other of soul-force; the one of hatred, the other of love; the one of disorder, the other of peace; one that is demoniac, the other that is godly. . . . We shall reap as we sow.[9]

Gandhi's conceptualization of freedom in Indian terms of swaraj *did not mean that he underrated western liberal ideals of political rights or social liberties. He wrote, "Freedom of speech and civil liberty are the very roots of* swaraj. *Without these the foundations of* swaraj *will remain weak."[10] Indeed, his effectiveness against the British came from his argument that they did not practice in India what their own political tradition preached. Gandhi held a law degree from London, practiced British law in South Africa successfully for thirteen years, and studied thoroughly the writings of English prophets of liberty like John Stuart Mill. He could shame the British by demanding respect for their own moral values, much as Martin Luther King, Jr., called on white Americans to fulfill democratic promises of equal opportunity.*

Gandhi elaborates basic liberties and rights in the following articles in ways that both challenge the British raj and lay the democratic foundations for a free India. His "Resolution on Fundamental Rights and Economic Changes" for the Indian National Congress, and extensive later commentary, represent a remarkable commitment to democratic values. Yet Gandhi did not stress rights at the cost of civic obligations. The last entry of this section contains an important element in this theory that "there is no duty but creates a corresponding right, and those only are true rights which flow from a due performance of one's duties." His idea of citizenship carried a strong element of social responsibility.

RESOLUTION ON FUNDAMENTAL RIGHTS AND ECONOMIC CHANGES

This Congress is of opinion that to enable the masses to appreciate what swaraj, as conceived by the Congress, will mean to them, it is desirable to state the position of the Congress in a manner easily understood by them. In order to end the exploitation of the masses, political freedom must include real economic freedom of the starving millions. The Congress, therefore, declare that any constitution which may be agreed to on its behalf should provide, or enable the Swaraj Government to provide for the following:

1. Fundamental rights of the people, including:
   (a) freedom of association and combination;
   (b) freedom of speech and of the Press;
   (c) freedom of conscience and the free profession and practice of religion, subject to public order and morality;
   (d) protection of the culture, language and scripts of the minorities;
   (e) equal rights and obligations of all citizens, without any bar on account of sex;
   (f) no disability to attach to any citizen by reason of his or her religion, caste or creed or sex in regard to public employment, office of power or honor and in the exercise of any trade or calling;
   (g) equal rights to all citizens in regard to public roads, wells, schools and other places of public resort;
   (h) right to keep and bear arms in accordance with regulations and reservations made in that behalf;

(i) no person shall be deprived of his liberty nor shall his dwelling or property be entered, sequestered or confiscated, save in accordance with law.

2. Religious neutrality on the part of the State.
3. Adult suffrage.
4. Free primary education.
5. A living wage for industrial workers, limited hours of labor, healthy conditions of work, protection against the economic consequences of old age, sickness and unemployment.
6. Labor to be freed from serfdom or conditions bordering on serfdom.
7. Protection of women workers, and specially adequate provisions for leave during maternity period.
8. Prohibition against employment of children of school-going age in factories.
9. Rights of labor to form unions to protect their interests with suitable machinery for settlement of disputes by arbitration.
10. Substantial reduction in agricultural rent or revenue paid by the peasantry, and in case of uneconomic holdings exemption from rent for such period as may be necessary, relief being given to small zamindars wherever necessary by reason of such reduction.
11. Imposition of a progressive income tax on agricultural incomes above a fixed minimum.
12. A graduated inheritance tax.
13. Military expenditure to be reduced by at least one half of the present scale.
14. Expenditure and salaries in civil departments to be largely reduced. No servant of the State, other than specially employed experts and the like, to be paid above a certain fixed figure which should not ordinarily exceed Rs. 500 per month.
15. Protection of indigenous cloth by exclusion of foreign cloth and foreign yarn from the country.
16. Total prohibition of intoxicating drinks and drugs.
17. No duty on salt manufactured in India.
18. Control over exchange and currency policy so as to help Indian industries and bring relief to the masses.
19. Control by the State of key industries and ownership of mineral resources.
20. Control of usury—direct or indirect.[11]

SPEECH ON FUNDAMENTAL RIGHTS

This resolution is meant for those who are not legislators, who are not interested in intricate questions of constitution, who will not take an active part in the administration of the country. It is meant to indicate to the poor, inarticulate Indian the broad features of swaraj. . . .

Clause 1(d) of the fundamental rights protect the culture, language and scripts of the minority. Now though I am sure that Islamic and Aryan cultures are not mutually exclusive and fundamentally different, I must recognize that Mussalmans look upon Islamic culture as distinctive from Aryan. Let us therefore cultivate tolerance. Let us try to learn the Urdu language and Urdu script and understand the Mussalmans' insistence on it.

Then there is the abolition of all disabilities attaching to women, in regard to public employment, office of power or honor, etc. The moment this is done many of the disabilities to which the women are subjected will cease. So far as the Congress is concerned, we have admitted no such disability. We have had Dr. Besant and Shrimati Sarojini Devi* as our presidents and in the future free State it will be open to us to have women presidents.

Religious neutrality is another important provision. Swaraj will favor Hinduism no more than Islam, nor Islam more than Hinduism. But in order that we may have a State based on religious neutrality, let us from now adopt the principle in our daily affairs. Let not a Hindu merchant hesitate to have deserving Muslims as his employees, and let every Congressman make religious neutrality his creed in every walk of life. . . .

Let the zamindars [landlords] and the Maharajas be assured that the Congress does not seek to destroy all wrong and injustice. Let them make an earnest endeavor to understand the grievances of their tenants and introduce adequate measures of relief before legislation overtakes them. . . .

Those who are opposed to the policy and principle must reject it, but they must bear in mind that the poor man's swaraj is soon coming and let them not be found unprepared when it actually comes [the resolution was passed].[12]

The resolution on fundamental rights is the most important resolution of the Congress. It shows what kind of swaraj the Congress wants to

*Dr. Annie Besant was president of the Indian National Congress in 1917, Sarojini Naidu, a distinguished poet, in 1925.

achieve. That swaraj is the poor man's swaraj or *Ramarajya*. Rama symbolized justice and equity, Rama symbolized truth and charity.

The resolution insists on religious toleration, which means, that no one
will be prevented from discharging his religious obligations, and the State
shall favor no religion.

Justice and equity mean the establishment of just and equitable relations between capital and labor, between the landlord and the tenant. The
landlord and the capitalist will cease to exploit the tenant and the laborer
but will studiously protect his interests.

Not that these things will be there as a matter of course as soon as we
get the powers. I only mean that they will follow as the natural conse-
quence of truth and non-violence if swaraj is achieved by those means.
The question is whether we are following truth and non-violence. *Ramarajya* cannot be the result of truth and non-violence followed as a mere
temporary expedient or policy. *Ramarajya* can only come out of truth and
non-violence pursued as a creed. Could a son ever fulfill his filial duties
as a policy? Policy is essentially a temporary expedient which one might
alter as circumstances altered. It is easy enough to follow truth and non-
violence so long as no sacrifice or suffering is involved, but he who ad-
heres to them in all circumstances even at the cost of life follows them as a
creed. It is time truth and non-violence were a creed and not policy with
us Congressmen.

Let us therefore find out what parts of the resolution we can enforce
even now. If we do not enforce the things that can be enforced today,
swaraj will be meaningless, for we will not suddenly do after swaraj things
which we can do but will not do today.

The resolution states that there shall be no untouchability under the
swaraj constitution. Have we cast out the canker of untouchability? The
resolution states that under the swaraj constitution there shall be no facilities for the licensing of liquor and drug shops. Have we cast out the drug
and drink evil from our midst? The resolution goes on to say that under
swaraj all foreign cloth would be banned from India. But have we given up
our infatuation with foreign cloth and become khaddar clad? Similarly
under swaraj, according to this resolution, Hindus and Mussalmans and
Christians will live together like true blood brothers. Have we cleansed
our hearts of distrust and suspicion of one another? Under swaraj, which
the resolution pictures, there shall be no hatred or ill-will between the
rich and the poor. Have the rich identified themselves with the poor, and
have the poor ceased to have ill-will toward the rich? Under the swaraj
constitution we want the maximum monthly emoluments of officials not

to exceed Rs. 500. But do those who are getting more today devote the balance to philanthropic purposes? Have our millionaires adjusted their standard of living to this scale of payment? It is difficult to give a decisive reply to these questions today. We are today slowly groping our way towards our ideal of Ramarajya or the Kingdom of Righteousness. This resolution is intended to keep this goal constantly before our eyes and to stimulate our endeavors to attain it.[13]

. . . National control of the Government is mostly dependent upon ourselves. Conversely if we do not do the things we ought to today, when the power comes to us we shall be found unready for them. Thus if we do not respect one another's religions, do not treat women as absolute equals, do not remove untouchability, do not dot villages with free primary schools, do not honestly manage the Congress suffrage which is practically adult suffrage, do not treat labor decently, do not spare children factory labor, do not encourage labor unions, do not reduce agricultural rents, do not pay for national purposes a fixed percentage of our incomes, do not voluntarily reduce our salaries or set apart for national purposes more than the minimum required, do not abjure foreign cloth and drink and do not reduce the heavy rates of interest which even respectable people charge, I prophecy that the State will be powerless to impose these reforms on an unwilling people. A popular State can never act in advance of public opinion. If it goes against it, it will be destroyed. Democracy disciplined and enlightened is the finest thing in the world. A democracy prejudiced, ignorant, superstitious will land itself in chaos and may be self-destroyed. The Fundamental Rights Resolution is not premature. It is not so formidable as it reads, if the nation is prepared, as I hold it is prepared, for orderly self-government. Let every Congressman therefore think out a program of work for himself or herself in terms of the items first mentioned. We need not be overpowered by the list. Each one may take up the item and the area of work for which he or she is best fitted. Needless to say the full working of the items requires the co-operation of capitalists, landowners and the like. They will all fall in line if a good beginning is made.[14]

Liberty of speech means that it is unassailed even when the speech hurts; liberty of the Press can be said to be truly respected only when the Press can comment in the severest terms upon and even misrepresent matters, protection against misrepresentation or violence being secured not by an administrative gagging order, not by closing down the Press but by punishing the real offender, leaving the Press itself unrestricted. Freedom of association is truly respected when assemblies of people can discuss even revolutionary projects, the State relying upon the force of public opinion and the civil police, not the savage military at its disposal, to crush any actual outbreak of revolution that is designed to confound public opinion and the State representing it.

The Government of India is now seeking to crush the three powerful vehicles of expressing and cultivating public opinion and is thus once more, but happily for the last time, proving its totally arbitrary and despotic character. The fight for swaraj, means fight for this threefold freedom before all else.

. . . The restoration of free speech, free association and free Press is almost the whole swaraj.[15]

In swaraj based on ahimsa people need not know their rights, but it is necessary for them to know their duties. There is no duty but creates a corresponding right, and those only are true rights which flow from a due performance of one's duties. Hence rights of true citizenship accrue only to those who serve the State to which they belong. And they alone can do justice to the rights that accrue to them. Everyone possesses the right to tell lies or resort to goondaism. But the exercise of such a right is harmful both to the exerciser and society. But to him who observes truth and non-violence comes prestige, and prestige brings rights. And people who obtain rights as a result of performance of duty, exercise them only for the service of society, never for themselves. Swaraj of a people means the sum total of the swaraj (self-rule) of individuals. And such swaraj comes only from performance by individuals of their duty as citizens. In it no one thinks of his rights. They come, when they are needed, for better performances of duty.[16]

Attainment of swaraj *therefore demanded performance of duty, or dharma, a position that Gandhi reinforces in the first entry that follows. Some Indian leaders argued that only after the nation achieved its independence from British rule could social reforms be achieved. Gandhi replied that the country needed to develop a spirit of civic responsibility, through social activism or commitment to the uplift of others, which could then make political independence truly meaningful. His message to those involved in the freedom struggle, therefore, was that they should work steadily on a specific agenda of social reforms that did not depend on the departure of the British, and he called this agenda his "constructive program."*

In the second article that follows, entitled "Implications of Constructive Programme," Gandhi lists thirteen items or areas of social and economic reform. The degree of attention that he gave to each depended on what he

*deemed most urgent during a particular phase of the movement, but he
consistently emphasized four that have also been selected for inclusion in this
section: Hindu-Muslim unity, removal of untouchability, uplift of women,
and working for economic equality. The selection here of these four obviously
does not demean the importance of the others. The readings have been
arranged in the order of his listing.*

*The first, Hindu-Muslim unity or the problem of resolving religious
tensions between India's Hindu majority and its large minority of eighty
million Muslims, was the issue that commanded Gandhi's greatest attention. Thus his first book, in 1909, gave more space to this than any other
question. As the excerpt here indicates, Gandhi believed that India's very
identity as a nation demanded an answer to it. He presents his analysis in
dialogue form between "Reader" and "Editor," with the second presenting his
own position.*

*Gandhi persisted until the last moments of his life in trying to resolve this
religious conflict. When one considers the decades of energy and thought that
he gave to this problem, emphasized especially by his Calcutta and Delhi
fasts, it is sad to conclude that the conflict was ultimately beyond his or
anyone's powers of resolution. Yet the failure does at least demonstrate his
point about social reforms: problems of religious conflict, caste prejudice,
sexual discrimination, and economic injustice all rank among the most
profound and persistent in India's long history.*

TRUE INDEPENDENCE

External freedom will always be the means of measuring the freedom of
the self within. Hence we often find that laws made to grant us freedom
often turn out to be shackles binding us. Hence the dharma of those workers who wish to attain true freedom is to try and attempt an improvement
in the self. If we understand this simple and straightforward fact, we shall
not even utter the word "legislature" but engage ourselves in constructive
activity [social reform] day and night. All can take part in such activity. It
is not necessary to become either a lawyer or a legislator in order to do so.
What strange blindness it is that those who are elected as legislators to
represent the people should seem, and in fact are, their rulers! If we are
not under an illusion, we would have no fear of the Government or the
legislatures, law-courts or the armies which subsist on it. And no power
can come in the way of our upliftment and our independence when we
have reformed ourselves in the above manner.[17]

IMPLICATIONS OF THE
CONSTRUCTIVE PROGRAMME

A correspondent writes:

> What are the qualities that you intend to inculcate in people by laying stress
> on the constructive programme? What are the qualifications necessary for a
> constructive worker in order to make his work effective?

The constructive programme is a big undertaking including a number of
items (1) Hindu-Muslim or communal unity; (2) Removal of untouchability; (3) Prohibition; (4) Khadi; (5) Other village industries; (6) Village sanitation; (7) New or basic education; (8) Adult education; (9) Uplift of
women; (10) Education in hygiene and health; (11) Propagation of Rashtrabhasha [national language]; (12) Cultivating love of one's own language;
(13) Working for economic equality. This list can be supplemented if necessary, but it is so comprehensive that I think it can be proved to include
items appearing to have been omitted.

The reader will see that it is the want of all these things that is responsible for our bondage.

. . . We have to stabilize and perfect ahimsa, and so we have to make the
constructive programme as comprehensive as possible. There should be
no room for doubt that, if we can win swaraj purely through non-violence,
we can also retain it through the same means. In the fulfillment of the
constructive programme lies the non-violent attainment of swaraj. . . .

Without Hindu-Muslim, i.e., communal unity, we shall always remain
crippled. And how can a crippled India win swaraj? Communal unity
means unity between Hindus, Sikhs, Mussalmans, Christians, Parsis,
Jews. All these go to make Hindustan. He who neglects any of these communities does not know constructive work.

As long as the curse of untouchability pollutes the mind of the Hindu,
so long is he himself an untouchable in the eyes of the world, and an untouchable cannot win non-violent swaraj. The removal of untouchability
means treating the so-called untouchables as one's own kith and kin. He
who does treat them so must be free from the sense of high and low, in fact
free from all wrong class-sense. He will regard the whole world as one
family. Under non-violent swaraj it will be impossible to conceive of any
country as an enemy country.

Pure swaraj is impossible of attainment by people who have been or
who are slaves of intoxicating drinks and drugs. It must never be forgot-

ten that a man in the grip of intoxicants is generally bereft of the moral sense.

Everyone now may be said to believe that without khadi there is no just and immediate solution of the problem of the starvation of our millions. I need not therefore dilate upon it. I would only add that in the resuscitation of khadi lies the resuscitation of the ruined village artisans. Khadi requisites (wheels, looms, etc.) have to be made by the village carpenter and blacksmith. For unless these requisites are made in the village it cannot be self-contained and prosperous.

The revival of khadi presupposes the revival of all other village industries. Because we have not laid proper stress on this, khadi-wearers see nothing wrong in using other articles which are foreign or mill-made. Such people may be said to have failed to grasp the inner meaning of khadi. They forget that by establishing the Village Industries Association the Congress has placed all other village industries on the same level as khadi. As the solar system will be dark without the sun, even so will the sun be lusterless without the planets. All things in the universe are interdependent. The salvation of India is impossible without the salvation of villages.

If rural reconstruction were not to include rural sanitation, our villages would remain the muck-heaps that they are today. Village sanitation is a vital part of village life and is as difficult as it is important. It needs a heroic effort to eradicate age-long insinuation. The village worker who is ignorant of the science of village sanitation, who is not a successful scavenger, cannot fit himself for village service.

It seems to be generally admitted that without the new or basic education the education of millions of children in India is well-nigh impossible. The village worker has, therefore, to master it, and become a basic education teacher himself.

Adult education will follow in the wake of basic education as a matter of course. Where this new education has taken root, the children themselves become their parents' teachers. Be that as it may, the village worker has to undertake adult education also.

Woman is described as man's better half. As long as she has not the same rights in law as man, as long as the birth of a girl does not receive the same welcome as that of a boy, so long we should know that India is suffering from partial paralysis. Suppression of woman is denial of ahimsa. Every village worker will, therefore, regard every woman as his mother, sister or daughter as the case may be, and look upon her with respect. Only such a worker will command the confidence of the village people.

It is impossible for an unhealthy people to win swaraj. Therefore we should no longer be guilty of the neglect of the health of our people. Every village worker must have a knowledge of the general principles of health.

Without a common language no nation can come into being. Instead of worrying himself with the controversy about the Hindi-Hindustani and Urdu, the village worker will acquire a knowledge of the *Rashtrabhasha*, which should be such as can be understood by both Hindus and Muslims.

Our infatuation about English has made us unfaithful to provincial languages. If only as penance for this unfaithfulness the village worker should cultivate in the villagers a love of their own speech. He will have equal regard for all the other languages of India, and will learn the language of the part where he may be working, and thus be able to inspire the villagers there with a regard for their speech.

The whole of this programme will, however, be a structure on sand if it is not built on the solid foundation of economic equality. Economic equality must never be supposed to mean possession of an equal amount of worldly goods by everyone. It does mean, however, that everyone will have a proper house to live in, sufficient and balanced food to eat, and sufficient khadi with which to cover himself. It also means that the cruel inequality that obtains today will be removed by purely non-violent means.[18]

HINDU-MUSLIM QUESTION IN INDIA

READER: You have described to me the India of the pre-Mahomedan period, but now we have Mahomedans, Parsis and Christians. How can they be one nation? Hindus and Mahomedans are old enemies. Our very proverbs prove it. Mahomedans turn to the West for worship, whilst Hindus turn to the East. The former look down on the Hindus as idolaters. The Hindus worship the cow, the Mahomedans kill her. The Hindus believe in the doctrine of non-killing, the Mahomedans do not. We thus meet with differences at every step. How can India be one nation?

EDITOR: India cannot cease to be one nation because people belonging to different religions live in it. The introduction of foreigners does not necessarily destroy the nation; they merge in it. A country is one nation only when such a condition obtains in it. That country must have a faculty for assimilation. India has ever been such a country. In reality, there are as many religions as there are individuals; but those who are conscious of the spirit of nationality do not interfere with one another's religion. If they do, they are not fit to be considered a nation. If the Hindus believe that India should be peopled only by Hindus, they are living in a dreamland. The

Hindus, the Mahomedans, the Parsis and the Christians who have made India their country are fellow countrymen, and they will have to live in unity, if only for their own interest. In no part of the world are one nationality and one religion synonymous terms; nor has it ever been so in India.

READER: But what about the inborn enmity between Hindus and Mahomedans?

EDITOR: That phrase has been invented by our mutual enemy. When the Hindus and Mahomedans fought against one another, they certainly spoke in that strain. They have long ceased to fight. How, then, can there be any inborn enmity? Pray remember this too, that we did not cease to fight only after British occupation. The Hindus flourished under Moslem sovereigns and Moslems under the Hindu. Each party recognized that mutual fighting was suicidal, and that neither party would abandon its religion by force of arms? Both parties, therefore, decided to live in peace. With the English advent quarrels re-commenced.

The proverbs you have quoted were coined when both were fighting; to quote them now is obviously harmful. Should we not remember that many Hindus and Mahomedans own the same ancestors and the same blood runs through their veins? Do people become enemies because they change their religion? Is the God of the Mahomedan different from the God of the Hindu? Religions are different roads converging to the same point. What does it matter that we take different roads so long as we reach the same goal? Wherein is the cause for quarreling?

Moreover, there are deadly proverbs as between the followers of Shiva and those of Vishnu, yet nobody suggests that these two do not belong to the same nation. It is said that the Vedic religion is different from Jainism, but the followers of the respective faiths are not different nations. The fact is that we have become enslaved and, therefore, quarrel and like to have our quarrels decided by a third party. There are Hindu iconoclasts as there are Mahomedan. The more we advance in true knowledge, the better we shall understand that we need not be at war with those whose religion we may not follow.

READER: Now I would like to know your views about cow-protection.

EDITOR: I myself respect the cow, that is, I look upon her with affectionate reverence. The cow is the protector of India because, being an agricultural country, she is dependent on the cow. The cow is a most useful animal in hundreds of ways. Our Mahomedan brethren will admit this.

But, just as I respect the cow, so do I respect my fellow-men. A man is just as useful as a cow no matter whether he be a Mahomedan or a Hindu.

Am I, then, to fight with or kill a Mahomedan in order to save a cow? In doing so, I would become an enemy of the Mahomedan as well as of the cow. Therefore, the only method I know of protecting the cow is that I should approach my Mahomedan brother and urge him for the sake of the country to join me in protecting her. If he would not listen to me I should let the cow go for the simple reason that the matter is beyond my ability. If I were overfull of pity for the cow, I should sacrifice my life to save her but not take my brother's. This, I hold, is the law of our religion.

When men become obstinate, it is a difficult thing. If I pull one way, my Moslem brother will pull another. If I put on superior airs, he will return the compliment. If I bow to him gently, he will do it much more so; and if he does not, I shall not be considered to have done wrong in having bowed. When the Hindus became insistent, the killing of cows increased. In my opinion, cow-protection societies may be considered cow-killing societies. It is a disgrace to us that we should need such societies. When we forgot how to protect cows, I suppose we needed such societies.

What am I to do when a blood-brother is on the point of killing a cow? Am I to kill him, or to fall down at his feet and implore him? If you admit that I should adopt the latter course, I must do the same to my Moslem brother.

Who protects the cow from destruction by Hindus when they cruelly ill-treat her? Whoever reasons with the Hindus when they mercilessly belabor the progeny of the cow with their sticks? But this has not prevented us from remaining one nation.

Lastly, if it be true that the Hindus believe in the doctrine of non-killing and the Mahomedans do not, what, pray, is the duty of the former? It is not written that a follower of the religion of Ahimsa (non-killing) may kill a fellow-man. For him the way is straight. In order to save one being, he may not kill another. . . .

READER: But will the English ever allow the two bodies to join hands?

EDITOR: This question arises out of your timidity. It betrays our shallowness. If two brothers want to live in peace, is it possible for a third party to separate them? If they were to listen to evil counsels we would consider them to be foolish. Similarly, we Hindus and Mahomedans would have to blame our folly rather than the English, if we allowed them to put us asunder. A clay pot would break through impact, if not with one stone, then with another. The way to save the pot is not to keep it away from the danger point but to bake it so that no stone would break it. Then we shall be steeled against all danger. This can be easily done by the Hindus.[19]

Liberty cannot be secured merely by proclaiming it. An atmosphere of liberty must be created within us. Liberty is one thing, and license another. Many a time we confuse license for liberty and lose the latter. License leads one to selfishness whereas liberty guides one to supreme good. License destroys society, liberty gives it life. In license propriety is sacrificed; in liberty it is fully cherished. Under slavery we practice several virtues out of fear; when liberated we practice them of our own free will. . . .

Therefore, if we have understood true freedom, we will shed communal fear. Hindus and Muslims will cease to fear one another. If both could shed fear at the same time all the better; but a free spirit should not expect the help of others to cast off fear. If the other side violates justice, even then he would not seek the help of a third party. He will depend only on his own strength, and if he loses, he will try to augment his own strength.[20]

HINDU-MUSLIM TENSION: ITS CAUSE AND CURE

Two years ago, a Mussalman friend said to me in all sincerity, "I do not believe [in] your non-violence. At least, I would not have my Mussalmans to learn it. Violence is the law of life. I would not have swaraj by non-violence as you define the latter. I must hate my enemy." This friend is an honest man. I entertain great regard for him. Much the same has been reported of another very great Mussalman friend of mine. The report may be untrue, but the reporter himself is not an untrue man.

Nor is this repugnance to non-violence confined to Mussalmans. Hindu friends have said the same thing, if possible, with greater vehemence. My claim to Hinduism has been rejected by some, because I believe [in] and advocate non-violence in its extreme form. They say that I am a Christian in disguise. I have been even seriously told that I am distorting the meaning of the Gita when I ascribe to that great poem the teaching of unadulterated non-violence. Some of my Hindu friends tell me that killing is a duty enjoyed by the Gita under certain circumstances. . . .

What I see around me today is, therefore, a reaction against the spread of non-violence. I feel the wave of violence coming. The Hindu-Muslim tension is an acute phase of this. . . .

If I am a Hindu, I cannot cease to be one even though I may be disowned by the whole of the Hindu population. I do, however, suggest that non-violence is the end of all religions. . . .

My strength lies in my asking people to do nothing that I have not tried repeatedly in my own life. I am then asking my countrymen today to adopt

non-violence as their final creed, only for the purpose of regulating the relations between the different races, and for the purpose of attaining
swaraj. Hindus and Mussalmans, Christians, Sikhs and Parsis must not
settle their differences by resort to violence, and the means for the attainment of swaraj must be non-violent. This I venture to place before India,
not as a weapon of the weak, but of the strong.[21]

For me the only question for immediate solution before the country is
the Hindu-Mussalman question. I agree with Mr. Jinnah [M. A. Jinnah, a
prominent Muslim leader] that Hindu-Muslim unity means swaraj. I see
no way of achieving anything in this afflicted country without a lasting
heart unity between Hindus and Mussalmans of India. I believe in the immediate possibility of achieving it, because it is so natural, so necessary for
both, and because I believe in human nature. Mussalmans may have much
to answer for. I have come in closest touch with even what may be considered a "bad lot." I cannot recall a single occasion when I had to regret it.
The Mussalmans are brave, they are generous and trusting the moment
their suspicion is disarmed. Hindus, living as they do in glass houses, have
no right to throw stones at their Mussalman neighbors. . . . The history of
Islam, if it betrays aberrations from the moral height, has many a brilliant
page. In its glorious days it was not intolerant. It commanded the admiration of the world. When the West was sunk in darkness, a bright star rose
in the Eastern firmament and gave light and comfort to a groaning world.
Islam is not a false religion. Let Hindus study it reverently and they will
love it even as I do. If it has become gross and fanatical here, let us admit
that we have had no small share in making it so. If Hindus set their house
in order, I have not a shadow of doubt that Islam will respond in a manner
worthy of its liberal traditions. The key to the situation lies with the Hindus. We must shed timidity or cowardice. We must be brave enough to
trust, all will be well.[22]

HINDU-MUSLIM UNITY

Everybody knows that without unity between Hindus and Mussulmans,
no certain progress can be made by the nation. There is no doubt that the
cement binding the two is yet loose and wet. There is still mutual distrust.
The leaders have come to recognize that India can make no advance without both feeling the need of trust and common action. But though there is
a vast change among the masses, it is still not a permanent quantity. The
Mussulman masses do not still recognize the same necessity for swaraj as

the Hindus do. The Mussulmans do not flock to public meetings in the same numbers of the Hindus. This process cannot be forced. Sufficient time has not passed for the national interest to be awakened among the Mussulmans. Indeed it is a marvel that whereas but a year ago the Mussulmans as a body hardly took any interest in Congress affairs, all over India thousands have registered themselves as members. This in itself is an immense gain.

But much more yet remains to be done. It is essentially the work of the Hindus. Wherever the Mussulmans are still found to be apathetic, they should be invited to come in. One often hears from Hindu quarters the complaint that Mussulmans do not join the Congress organizations or do not pay to the Swaraj Fund. The natural question is, have they been invited? In every district Hindus must make special efforts to draw out their Mussulman neighbors. There will never be real equality so long as one feels inferior or superior to the other. There is no room for patronage among equals. Mussulmans must not feel the lack of education or numbers where they are in a minority. Deficiency in education must be corrected by taking education. To be in a minority is often a blessing. Superiority in numbers has frequently proved a hindrance. It is character that counts in the end. . . .

To my Mussulman friends I would but say one word. They must not be irritated by the acts of irresponsible or ignorant but fanatical Hindus. He who exercises restraint under provocation wins the battle.[23]

As soon as I heard that the Hindus and Mussulmans of Nellore were at sixes and sevens, I thought of coming and remaining in your midst for some time. I wanted to know who those Hindus and who those Mussulmans were who would rather quarrel amongst themselves and retard the attainment of swaraj. . . . I have not come here to judge between my Hindu and Mussulman brethren. But as an expert on Hindu and Muslim unity, I propose in all humility to place, for your consideration and acceptance, certain fundamental principles on which, and on which alone, such a unity can remain everlasting. As a *Sanatana* Dharma Hindu, feeling for my own faith, hoping that if the Faith was on its trial, I would be found in the front rank to give my life for its sake as a *Sanatani* Hindu, I wish first of all to address myself to my Hindu brethren, and would say: "If you would live in amity and friendship with the Mohammedan countrymen, the only way you can do so is never on any account to put a strain upon their religious fervor and always yield to them even though you may consider that their demands are unreasonable and unjust. But there is a condition attached

to that submission even to unreasonable demands and that condition is
that their demands do not encroach upon the vital part of your religious
tenets."

. . . The test for friendship, the test for brotherhood is that each party
always makes allowances for the weaknesses of the other and I know that
on the Judgment Day that party will win the day which will be able to
show that it has always surrendered on non-essentials. The life of the
great Prophet is for you as a living example of a perpetual surrender of
non-essentials. But I say to the Hindu and Mussulman brethren of Nellore, whether they can agree about their differences or not, whether they
can make concessions to one another or not, whether they can come to an
agreement on essentials and non-essentials or not, it is not given to them,
not to a single Hindu or to a single Mussulman to fly at each other's
throats, to throw stones at one another, and to inflict violence on one another. They must have trusted, chosen leaders of each community to form
a Board of Arbitration to settle all religious disputes between the two. . . .

Let Hindus and Mussulmans understand firmly that the cornerstone
of swaraj, the cornerstone of the freedom of India is Hindu and Muslim
unity.[24]

How do you propose to solve the Hindu-Muslim problem?

By constantly insisting upon both the communities cultivating mutual
respect and trust and by insisting upon Hindus surrendering out of
strength to the Mussalman in every mundane matter and by showing that
those who claim to be nationalists and are in an overwhelming majority
should stand out in any unseemly competition for legislative or administrative control. I hope also to achieve the end by demonstrating that real
swaraj will come not by the acquisition of authority by a few but by the acquisition of the capacity by all to resist authority when it is abused. In
other words, swaraj is to be attained by educating the masses to a sense of
their capacity to regulate and control authority.[25]

Hindu-Muslim unity is possible if only we have mutual toleration,
and faith in ourselves and therefore in the ultimate goodness of human
nature.[26]

I came to the conclusion long ago, after prayerful search and study and
discussion with as many people as I could meet, that all religions were true
and also that all had some error in them, and that whilst I hold by my own,
I should hold others as dear as Hinduism, from which it logically follows
that we should hold all as dear as our nearest kith and kin and that we
should make no distinction between them. So we can only pray, if we are

Hindus, not that a Christian should become a Hindu, or if we are Mussalmans, not that a Hindu or a Christian should become a Mussalman, nor should we even secretly pray that anyone should be converted, but our inmost prayer should be that a Hindu should be a better Hindu, a Muslim a better Muslim and a Christian a better Christian. That is the fundamental truth of fellowship.[27]

When Gandhi attacked the traditional institutions of caste and untouchability, he opposed ancient pillars of his religion. He knew the extent of the social change that he demanded. "It is the whole of Hinduism that has to be purified and purged," he declared. "What I am aiming at is the greatest reform of the age."[28] The caste system, unique to India, dates back to the beginnings of Hinduism in 1500 B.C. As a theory of social organization, it conceived that Indian society is divided into four major groups or varnas: brahmins, kshatriyas, vaishyas, and sudras, representing and performing the functions respectively of spiritual authority, political power, commercial activity, and manual labor. Rigid hierarchical stratification of these vast groups and their innumerable subcastes was enforced through strict prohibitions on intermarriage and eating at the same table, or "inter-dining." Outside of the caste system was the lowest order of Hindu society, the untouchables, approximately 12 percent of the population in Gandhi's time. This group, despised and isolated, were regarded as contaminated because their assigned duties included handling unclean objects or collecting garbage and human waste. Gandhi called the untouchables harijans *or "children of God," and although he was born of the* vaishya *caste, he counted himself among the* harijans. *From the outset of his national leadership, he insisted that the abolition of untouchability must be a major goal of the independence movement and that* swaraj *could never be attained without this reform.*

In this respect Gandhi failed, because caste and untouchability persist in India today, but the following writings signify his unqualified efforts in this direction. As the initial brief entry indicates, he first ensured that all elements of caste and untouchability were eliminated in his own ashram, the small spiritual community that he had established in Ahmedabad, Gujarat. The ashram served as a model for the egalitarian society that he believed India could become. Any reform that Gandhi wanted was first tested in his ashram. The following articles in this section indicate how he presented the issue in resolutions before the Indian National Congress, speeches throughout India, and the columns of his weekly newspaper, the name of which he changed in 1933 from Young India *to* Harijan.

Caste distinctions are not respected in the Ashram because they are not part of dharma. They have no connection with the Hindu dharma. It is sinful to regard anybody as higher or lower. All of us are equal. We are polluted by sin, never by human beings. One who wishes to serve cannot look upon anybody as higher or lower. The belief in such distinctions is a blot on Hinduism. We should remove it.[29]

THE SIN OF UNTOUCHABILITY

It is worthy to note that the Subjects Committee [of the National Congress, 1920] accepted without any opposition the clause regarding the sin of untouchability. It is well that the National assembly passed the resolution stating that the removal of this blot on Hinduism was necessary for the attainment of swaraj. The devil succeeds only by receiving help from his fellows. He always takes advantage of the weakest spots in our natures in order to gain mastery over us. Even so does the Government retain its control over us through our weaknesses or vices. And if we would render ourselves proof against its machinations we must remove our weaknesses. It is for that reason that I have called non-co-operation a process of purification. As soon as that process is completed, this Government must fall to pieces for want of the necessary environment, just as mosquitoes cease to haunt a place whose cesspools are filled up and dried.

Has not a just Nemesis overtaken us for the crime of untouchability? Have we not reaped as we have sown? Have we not practiced Dyerism and O'Dwyerism on our own kith and kin? We have segregated the "pariah" and we are in turn segregated in the British Colonies. We deny him the use of public wells; we throw the leavings of our plates at him. His very shadow pollutes us. Indeed there is no charge that the "pariah" cannot fling in our faces and which we do not fling in the faces of Englishmen.

How is this blot on Hinduism to be removed? "Do unto others as you would that others should do unto you." I have often told English officials that, if they are friends and servants of India, they should come down from their pedestal, cease to be patrons, demonstrate by their loving deeds that they are in every respect our friends, and believe us to be equals in the same sense they believe fellow-Englishmen to be their equals . . . to repent and to change their hearts. Even so it is necessary for us Hindus to repent of the wrong we have done, to alter our behavior towards those whom we have "suppressed" by a system as devilish as we believe the English system of the Government of India to be. We must not throw a few miserable schools at them: we must not adopt the air of superiority towards them.

We must treat them as our blood-brothers as they are in fact. We must return to them the inheritance of which we have robbed them. And this must not be the act of a few English-knowing reformers merely, but it must be a conscious voluntary effort on the part of the masses. We may not wait till eternity for this much belated reformation. We must aim at bringing it about within this year of grace, probation, preparation, and *tapasya*. It is a reform not to follow swaraj but to precede it.

Untouchability is not a sanction of religion, it is a device of Satan. The devil has always quoted scriptures. But scriptures cannot transcend reason and truth. They are intended to purify reason and illuminate truth. . . . For me the Vedas are divine and unwritten. "The letter killeth." It is the spirit that giveth the light. And the spirit of the Vedas is purity, truth, innocence, chastity, humility, simplicity, forgiveness, godliness, and all that makes a man or woman noble and brave. There is neither nobility nor bravery in treating the great and uncomplaining scavengers [untouchables] of the nation as worse than dogs to be despised and spat upon. Would that God gave us the strength and the wisdom to become voluntary scavengers of the nation as the "suppressed" classes are forced to be. There are Augean stables enough and to spare for us to clean.[30]

[A correspondent asks:] I am unable to understand the relation between the existence of this evil [of untouchability] and the establishment of swaraj. After all, "unapproachability" is only one of the many evils of the Hindu society—perhaps a greater evil—and as long as society exists similar evils do exist, as no society is free from evils. How is this an impediment to the obtaining of swaraj and why do you make its removal a condition precedent to our fitness for swaraj? . . . No amount of external embracing will ease the situation, unless the spirit of toleration exists within.

I abhor with my whole soul the system which has reduced a large number of Hindus to a level less than that of beasts. The vexed problem would be solved if the poor *Panchama* [untouchable] was allowed to mind his own business. Unfortunately, he has no mind or business he can call his own. Has a beast any mind or business but that of his master's? Has a *Panchama* a place he can call his own? He may not walk on the very roads he cleans and pays for by the sweat of his brow. He may not even dress as the others do. The correspondent talks of toleration. It is an abuse of language to say that we Hindus extend any toleration towards our *Panchama* brothers. We have degraded them and then have the audacity to use their very degradation against their rise.

Swaraj for me means freedom for the meanest of our countrymen. If the lot of the *Panchama* is not improved when we are all suffering, it is not likely to be better under the intoxication of swaraj. If it is necessary for us to buy peace with the Mussalmans as a condition of swaraj, it is equally necessary for us to give peace to the *Panchama* before we can, with any show of justice or self-respect, talk of swaraj. I am not interested in freeing India merely from the English yoke. I am bent upon freeing India from any yoke whatsoever. I have no desire to exchange King Log for King Stork. Hence for me the movement of swaraj is a movement of self-purification.[31]

I must say that the service of the so-called untouchables does not rank with me as in any way subordinate to any kind of political work. Just a moment ago I met two missionary friends who drew the same distinction and therefore came in for some gentle rebuke from me. I suggested to them that my work of social reform was in no way less than or subordinate to political work. The fact is, that when I saw that to a certain extent my social work would be impossible without the help of political work, I took to the latter and only to the extent that it helped the former. I must therefore confess that work of social reform or self-purification of this nature is a hundred times dearer to me than what is called purely political work.

For what does service of the "untouchables" or rendering justice to them mean? It means nothing less than redeeming a debt which is centuries overdue, and to expiate in some measure the sin we have been guilty of for ages, viz., that of oppressing and insulting our own kith and kin. We have behaved towards these unfortunate brethren of ours nothing better than a man turned monster behaves towards brother man. And the program of removal of untouchability that we have set before us is just some little expiation for a monstrous wrong. And as it is essentially by way of expiation or self-purification, it cannot be prompted by any fear of favor. If we take up this work, fearing that the so-called untouchables would go over to another faith, or that they would wreak vengeance on us, or as a sort of political trump card, we shall have betrayed our ignorance of Hinduism and our ungratefulness to those who have served us for ages. I admit that it was I who pushed the item to the forefront of the Congress program, and anyone bent on cavilling at me might say that it was a clever bait held out by me to the untouchables. Let me say at once that charge is idle. It grew on me very early in life that those who believed themselves to be Hindus must perform the penance in the shape of wiping out this stain before they could be proud of Hinduism, and as the majority of Congressmen were Hindus, and as the program then put before the nation was not one of self-purification, I put it in the forefront of the Congress program, in the conviction that unless the Hindus were prepared to wipe out this stain they could not regard themselves as fit for swaraj. That conviction has come upon me as a self-evident proposition. If we came into power, with the stain of untouchability unfazed, I am positive that the untouchables would be far worse under that "swaraj" than they are now, for the simple reason that our weaknesses and our failings would then be buttressed up by the accession of power. That in brief is my position, and I have always held that self-purification is an indispensable condition of swaraj. It is not a position that I have arrived at today. It is as old as when I began to think of swaraj. That is why I thank God for enabling me to participate in this function today. I have always prized opportunities for doing this kind of work, and have often put aside so-called political work for work of this nature. I know that those to whom only the exciting thing called "politics" has an exclusive appeal will laugh at this kind of thing. But for me it is nearest and dearest to my heart.[32]

AN IMPATIENT WORKER

An earnest but impatient worker has been trying to have temples and public places thrown open to Harijans. He had some success but nothing to be proud of. In his impatience, therefore, he writes:

> It is no use waiting for these orthodox men to make a beginning. They will never move unless compelled to do so. Drastic steps are required to wipe off untouchability. I therefore beg you to kindly favor me with your opinion if satyagraha at the entrance of the temples by workers and Harijans preventing orthodox persons from entering the temples will be an effective method. Appeals and entreaties have produced no effect, and to lose more time on these will, in my humble opinion, be sheer waste of valuable time.

Such blocking the way will be sheer compulsion. And there should be no compulsion in religion or in matters of any reform. The movement for the removal of untouchability is one of self-purification. No man can be purified against his will. Therefore, there can be no force directly or indirectly used against the orthodox. If should be remembered that many of us were like the orthodox people before our recognition of the necessity of the removal of untouchability. We would not then have liked anybody to block our way to the temples, because we in those days believed, no doubt wrongly as we now think, that harijans should not be allowed to enter temples. Even so may we not block the way of the orthodox to the temples.

I should also remind correspondents that the word "satyagraha" is often most loosely used and is made to cover veiled violence. But as the author of the word I may be allowed to say that it excludes every form of violence, direct or indirect, veiled or unveiled, and whether in thought, word or deed. It is a breach of satyagraha to wish ill to an opponent or to say a harsh word to him or of him with the intention of harming him. And often the evil thought or the evil word may, in terms of satyagraha, be more dangerous than actual violence used in the heat of the moment and perhaps repented and forgotten the next moment. Satyagraha is gentle, it never wounds. It must not be the result of anger or malice. It is never fussy, never impatient, never vociferous. It is the direct opposite of compulsion. It was conceived as a complete substitute for violence.

Nevertheless, I fully agree with the correspondent that "most drastic steps are required to wipe off untouchability." But these steps have to be taken against ourselves. The orthodox people sincerely believe that untouchability, as they practice it, is enjoined by the Shastras [sacred texts] and that great evil will befall them and Hinduism if it was removed. How is one to cope with this belief? It is clear that they will never change their belief by being compelled to admit Harijans to their temples. What is required is not so much of the entry of Harijans to the temples as the conversion of the orthodox to the belief that it is wrong to prevent Harijans from entering the temples. This conversion can only be brought about by an appeal to their hearts, i.e., by evoking the best that is in them. Such an appeal can be made by the appellants' prayers, fasting and other suffering in their own persons, in other words, by their ever-increasing purity. It has never yet been known to fail. For it is its own end. The reformer must have consciousness of the truth of his cause. He will not then be impatient with the opponent, he will be impatient with himself. He must be prepared even to fast unto death. Not everyone has the right or the capacity to do so. God is most exacting. He exacts humility from His votaries. Even fasts may take the form of coercion. But there is nothing in the world that in human hands does not lend itself to abuse. The human being is a mixture of good and evil, Jekyll and Hyde. But there is the least likelihood of abuse when it is a matter of self-suffering.[33]

SPEECH AT PUBLIC MEETING, TRICHINOPOLY

In the evening of my life I am not likely to take up a sectional cause to the injury of the public cause. And if at the present moment I appear to be advocating a sectional cause, you may depend upon it that behind that sectional cause lies deep down the desire that the whole of the public may benefit by it. For I do not believe that life is divided into separate air-tight compartments. On the contrary it is an undivided and indivisible whole; and, therefore, what is or may be good for one must be good for all. Whatever activity fails to stand that unmistakable test is an activity that must be abjured by all who have the public weal at heart.

Having throughout my life believed in this doctrine of universal good, never have I taken up any activity—be it sectional or national—which would be detrimental to the good of humanity as a whole. And in pursuing that universal goal, I discovered years ago that untouchability, as it is practiced today among Hindus, is a hindrance not only to the march of Hindus towards their own good, but also a hindrance to the general good of all. He who runs may discover for himself how this untouchability has taken in its snaky coil not merely caste Hindus but all other communities representing different faiths in India, that is to say, Mussalmans, Christians and others. In dealing with the monster of untouchability my own innermost desire is not that the brotherhood of Hindus only may be achieved, but it essentially is that the brotherhood of man—be he Hindu, Mussalman, Christian, Parsi or Jew—may be realized. For I believe in the fundamental truth of all great religions of the world. I believe that they are all God-given, and I believe that they were necessary for the people to whom these religions were revealed. And I believe that, if only we could all of us read the scriptures of the different faiths from the standpoint of the followers of those faiths we should find that they were at bottom all one and were all helpful to one another.

Hence it is that I have not hesitated to ask all non-Hindus to help me with their prayer in this mission, and it is because I have a living faith in my mission and because that faith is based on an extensive experience that I have not hesitated to say with the greatest deliberation that, if we, Hindus, do not destroy this monster of untouchability, it will devour both Hindus and Hinduism. And when I ask you to purify your hearts of untouchability, I ask of you nothing less than this—that you should believe in the fundamental unity and equality of man. I invite you all to forget that there are any distinctions of high and low among the children of one and the same God.

And therefore it is that I have not hesitated to plead on bended knees before those caste Hindus who call themselves sanatanists [orthodox] that they should join hands with me in this movement of self-purification. If they would only patiently study it and its implications, they would discover that there are more points of contact than of difference between them and the reformers. They cannot possibly, if they will study the movement, justify themselves in subjecting to indignities all those who are considered untouchables.[34]

I am essentially a lover of peace. I do not have the slightest wish to create dissensions among the Hindus. It would be best for the sanatanists and reformers to confer among themselves and make an effort to arrive at an understanding. But if that effort fails, both parties should resort to peaceful and honorable methods and both should learn to tolerate one another. I believe myself to be both a sanatanist and a reformer. I have tried to gather in me all the goodwill which caste Hindus can have towards Harijans. God alone knows how far I have succeeded in this effort. I am also trying, as best as an imperfect human being like myself can, to see with Harijans' eyes and to realize what is going on in their hearts. It is not given to man to know the whole truth. His duty lies in living up the truth as he sees it and, in doing so, to resort to the purest means, i.e., to non-violence. I do not want to hurt the feelings of the sanatanists. I want to convert them to my view in the gentlest manner. I want, if I can, to steal into their hearts. I would love to melt their hearts by my suffering. I firmly believe that untouchability as we practice it today has no sanction in the Shastras. But I do not wish to enter into a discussion of what the Shastras support and what they do not. I only put before you, as humbly as I can, the truth as I see it, and am prepared to sacrifice my life, if need be, in an unceasing effort to live up to that truth. It is clear to my mind, beyond the shadow of a doubt, that, if untouchability is not eradicated, both Hinduism and the Hindus are bound to perish. Ever since I was a child of ten I have considered untouchability as a sin. My heart has never been able to reconcile itself to untouchability based on birth. I tried to study the Shastras to the best of my ability. I consulted as many pundits as I could. And a majority of them have supported my view. But truth is not to be found in books. Truth resides in every human heart, and one has to search for it there, and be guided by truth as one sees it. But no one has a right to coerce others to act according to his own view of truth.

I would appeal to the temple-goers here who are in favor of Harijans' entry into the temple to go into the temple only after the sanatanists, who have blocked the way, leave the place. We do not want to score a victory over them. Do not be angry with them, do not insult them; on the contrary, feed them if they are hungry and would accept your hospitality. We have to win them over by love.[35]

CASTE HAS TO GO

My own position has been often stated in these columns. It may be summed up as follows:

1. I believe in varnashrama [four social orders] of the Vedas which in my opinion is based on absolute equality of status, notwithstand-

ing passages to the contrary in the *smritis* [sacred texts] and elsewhere.

2. Every word of the printed works passing muster as "Shastras" is
   not, in my opinion, a revelation.

3. The interpretation of accepted texts has undergone evolution, and
   is capable of indefinite evolution, even as the human intellect and
   heart are.

4. Nothing in the Shastras which is manifestly contrary to universal
   truths and morals can stand.

5. Nothing in the Shastras which is capable of being reasoned can
   stand if it is in conflict with reason.

6. Varnashrama of the Shastras is today non-existent in practice.

7. The present caste system is the very antithesis of varnashrama.
   The sooner public opinion abolishes it the better.

8. In varnashrama there was and should be no prohibition of intermarriage or inter-dining. Prohibition there is of change of one's
   hereditary occupation for purposes of gain. The existing practice
   is, therefore, doubly wrong in that it has set up cruel restrictions
   about inter-dining and intermarriage and tolerates anarchy about
   choice of occupation.

9. Though there is in varnashrama no prohibition against intermarriage and inter-dining, there can be compulsion. It must be left to
   the unfettered choice of the individual as to where he or she will
   marry or dine. If the law of varnashrama was observed there would
   naturally be a tendency, as far as marriage is concerned, for people
   to restrict the marital relations to their own varna.

10. As I have repeatedly said there is no such thing as untouchability
    by birth in the Shastras. I hold the present practice to be a sin and
    the greatest blot on Hinduism. I feel more than ever that if un-
    touchability lives, Hinduism dies.

11. The most effective, quickest, and the most unobtrusive way to de-
    stroy caste is for reformers to begin the practice with themselves
    and where necessary take the consequences of social boycott. The
    reform will not come by reviling the orthodox. The change will be
    gradual and imperceptible. The so-called higher classes will have
    to descend from their pedestal before they can make any impres-
    sion upon the so-called lower classes. Day-to-day experience of
    village work shows how difficult the task is of bridging the gulf
    that exists between the city-dwellers and the villagers, the higher
    classes and the lower classes. The two are not synonymous terms.
    For the class distinction exists both in the cities and the villages.[36]

So far as Harijans are concerned, every Hindu should make common cause with them and befriend them in their awful isolation—such isolation as perhaps the world has never seen in the monstrous immensity one witnesses in India. I know from experience how difficult the task is. But it is part of the task of building the edifice of swaraj. And the road to swaraj is steep and narrow. There are many slippery ascents and many deep chasms. They have all to be negotiated with unfaltering step before we can reach the summit and breathe the fresh air of freedom.[37]

Gandhi consistently featured the "uplift of women" in his program of social reforms. The political advantages of this became painfully obvious to the British government as women participated actively in civil-disobedience campaigns. But the aim of women's emancipation was part of a broader effort that went beyond politics. Gandhi believed that at every level of national development, the country must draw on the energy and ability of its female population. He had begun this cause in South Africa, arguing as early as 1907 for women's education. "Indian men," he declared then, "have deliberately kept their women backward," and "if this state of affairs continues, India will remain in its present abominable condition even if she were to secure all her rights from the British Government."[38] Thirty years later, after mobilizing millions of women as nonviolent resisters in successive satyagrahas, *Gandhi spoke before the All-India Women's Conference, declaring that* swaraj *and "the progress of India in all directions [are] impossible" without the advancement of women: "When woman whom we call* abala *[weak] becomes* sabala *[strong], all those who are helpless will become powerful."[39]*

The first entry that follows, "Untouchability, Women and Swaraj," indicates the connections in Gandhi's thought among essential social reforms and how swaraj *depends on the "inward growth" necessary to tackle these problems successfully.*

UNTOUCHABILITY, WOMEN AND SWARAJ

The question of breaking down the feminine prejudice is most difficult. It is in reality a question of female education. And in this it is a question not merely of education of girls but it is one of the education of married women. I have therefore repeatedly suggested that every patriotic husband should become the wife's own teacher and prepare her for work among her less fortunate sisters. I have also drawn attention to the implications of the suggestion. One of them is for husbands to cease to treat their wives as objects of their enjoyment but to regard them as co-partners in their work of nation-building. . . .

That freedom which is associated with the term swaraj in the popular mind is no doubt unattainable without not only the removal of untouchability and the promotion of heart unity between the different sections but also without removing many other social evils that can be easily named. That inward growth which must never stop we have come to understand by the comprehensive term swaraj. And that swaraj cannot be had so long as walls of prejudice, passion and superstition continue to stifle the growth of that stately oak.[40]

SPEECH AT BHAGINI SAMAJ, BOMBAY

Dear Sisters and Brothers of Bhagini Samaj,

I am thankful to you for asking me to preside over this annual function of the Samaj [Women's Association]. Your president, I really feel, should be a woman, though you may seek men's help or advice in your work. The Samaj is dedicated to the noble aim of women's regeneration and, in the same way that another's *tapascharya* [self-sacrifice] does not help one to ascend to heaven, man cannot bring about the regeneration of women. I don't mean to suggest that men do not desire it, or that women would not want to have it through men's help; I merely wish to place before you the principle that it is only through self-help that an individual or race can rise. This is not a new principle, but we often forget to act upon it.

The Samaj is at present kept going by the enthusiasm of Bhai Karsandas Chitalia. I am looking forward to a time when one of you will take his place and release him from this Samaj for other work. Having dedicated his life wholly to the service of women, he will find out some work in the same field. The Samaj will come into its own when it elects its office-bearers from among its women members and gives a better account of itself than it does today. I have close associations, as you know, with both men and women, but I find that I can do nothing in the way of service to women without help from women workers. That is why I take every occasion to protest in no uncertain terms that, so long as women in India remain ever so little suppressed or do not have the same rights [as men], India will not make real progress. Hence it will be all to India's honor if this Samaj succeeds completely in its aims.

It is necessary to understand what we mean when we talk of the regeneration of women. It presupposes degeneration and, if that is so, we should further consider what led to it and how. It is our primary duty to have some very hard thinking on these points. In travelling all over India, I have come to realize that all the existing agitation is confined to an infinitesimal section of our people who are really a mere speck in the vast firmament. Crores [1 crore = 10 million] of people of both the sexes live in absolute ignorance of this agitation. Full 85 percent of the people of this country pass their innocent days in a state of total detachment from what is going on around them. These men and women, ignorant as they are, do their bit in life well and properly. Both have the same education or, rather, the absence of education, both are helping each other as they ought to do. If their lives are in any sense incomplete, the cause can be traced to the incompleteness of the lives of the remaining 15 percent. If my sisters of the Bhagini Samaj will make a close study of the lives of the 85 percent of our people, it will provide them ample material for an excellent program of work for the Samaj.

In the observations that I am going to make, I will confine myself to the 15 percent above mentioned and, even then, it would be out of place to discuss the disabilities that are common both to men and women. The point for us to consider is the degeneration of our women relatively to our men. Legislation has been mostly the handiwork of men; and man has not always been fair and discriminate in performing that self-appointed task.

What the authors of the various *smritis* have said about women can in no wise be defended. Child-marriage, the restrictions on widows and such other evils owe their origin to the injunctions in the *smritis*. Women's being placed on a level with Sudras [servant class] has done unimaginable harm to Hindu society. These statements of mine may have verbal similarity with the occasional attacks of Christians, but, apart from this similarity, there is no other common ground between us. The Christians, in their attacks, seek to strike at the roots of Hinduism. I look upon myself as an orthodox Hindu and my attack proceeds from the desire to rid Hinduism of its defects and restore it to its pristine glory. The Christian critic, by demonstrating the imperfection of the *smritis*, tries to show that they are just ordinary books. My attempt is to show that the imperfection of the *smritis* comes from interpolated passages, that is to say, verses inserted by persons accepted as *smritikaras* [authors of smritis] in the period of our degeneration. It is easy to demonstrate the grandeur of the smritis minus these verses. I do not have the slightest desire to put up a weak defense of Hinduism, believing out of false pride or in ignorance, and wanting others to believe, that there is no error in the smritis or in the other accepted books of the Hindu religion. I am convinced that such an effort will not raise the Hindu religion but will degrade it rather. A religion which gives the foremost place to truth can afford no admixture of untruth.

The largest part of our effort in promoting the regeneration of women should be directed towards removing those blemishes which are represented in our shastras as the necessary and ingrained characteristics of women. Who will attempt this and how? In my humble opinion, in order to make the attempt we will have to produce women, pure, firm and self-controlled as Sita, Damayanti and Draupadi [heroines of ancient India]. If we do produce them, such modern sisters will receive the same homage from Hindu society as is being paid to their prototypes of yore. Their words will have the same authority as the shastras. We will feel ashamed of the stray reflections on them in our *smritis* and will soon forget them. Such revolutions have occurred in Hinduism in the past and will still take place in the future, leading to the stability of our faith. I pray to God that this Samaj might soon produce such women as I have described above.

We have now discussed the root cause of the degeneration of our women and have considered the ideals by the realization of which the present condition of our women can be improved. The number of women who can realize those ideals will be necessarily very few and, therefore, we will now consider what ordinary women can accomplish if they will try. Their first attempt should be directed towards awakening in the minds of as many women as possible a proper sense of their present condition. I am not among those who believe that such an effort can be made through literary education only. To work on that basis would be to postpone indefinitely the accomplishment of our aims; I have experienced at every step that it is not at all necessary to wait so long. We can bring home to our women the sad realities of their present condition without, in the first instance, giving them any literary education.

I am just returning from a district of Bihar. I once met there a large group of women from respectable families of the place. They all observed purdah. In my presence, they removed the purdah as they would in the presence of a brother. These women had had no education. Just before I went to meet them, an English woman had been to see me. She had called on me where I sat surrounded by a number of men. To meet the Hindu women, on the other hand, I had to go into a room specially set apart. Half seriously, I suggested that we could go to the room where the men were sitting. All enthusiasm, they said that they would be only too happy to do so, but that the custom being what it was, they would need the men's permission. They did not like the purdah at all [they said] and wanted me to see that the custom was ended. While there is tragedy in these words, they also bear out what I have said above. These women had realized their condition without having had any literary education. They were right in asking my help, but I wanted them to have the strength themselves to win their freedom and they admitted, too, that they had such strength. I have come away full of hope that we shall soon hear that these women have flung away the purdah. Women who would ordinarily be considered uneducated are doing excellent work in Champaran. They are waking up their extremely backward sisters to the freedom which they themselves enjoy.

Woman is the companion of man, gifted with equal mental capacities. She has the right to participate in the very minutest detail in the activities of man and she has an equal right of freedom and liberty with him. She is entitled to a supreme place in her own sphere of activity as man is in his. This ought to be the natural condition of things and not as a result only of learning to read and write. By sheer force of a vicious custom, even the most ignorant and worthless men have been enjoying a superiority over women which they do not deserve and ought not to have. Many of our movements stop half-way because of the condition of our women. Much of our work does not yield appropriate results; our lot is like that of the penny-wise and pound-foolish trader who does not employ enough capital in his business.

If I am right, a good many from among you, members of this Samaj, should go out to educate your ignorant sisters about their real condition. In practical terms, this means that you should spare as much time as you can to visit the most backward localities in Bombay and give the women there what you have yourselves received. If you have joined men in their religious, political and social activities, acquaint them with these. If you have gained any special knowledge about the bringing up of children, impart it to them. If you have studied and realized in your own experience the benefits of clean air, clean water, clean and simple food, and exercise, tell these women about them too. In this way, you will raise yourselves and them.[41]

WOMEN OF GUJARAT

How can women stand aside from a movement which is inspired by such great hopes? I have, therefore, been requesting women to come forward and take part in it. It is these hopes, I think, which have roused women throughout the country.

But should I, trusting to this enthusiasm, advise women to go to jail? I feel that I cannot do otherwise. If I did not encourage them to do so, that would be a reflection on my faith in them. A *yajna* is incomplete without women taking part in it. Fearlessness is just as essential for women as it is for men. I thought, therefore, that it would be good if women give their signatures and get used to the idea of going to jail. It also occurred to me that if women ceased being frightened by the thought of jail, it would be easier for men to court arrest.[42]

The last component considered here of Gandhi's program of social reforms is what he called "working for economic equality." He gave to his theory of economics the term sarvodaya, *which means literally "the welfare of all." He wanted to establish conceptual connections among the ideas of individual or national freedom, nonviolent action for social reforms, and economic equality, the last achieved mainly through a just distribution of wealth. He spoke, therefore, of the relationship of* swaraj *to* satyagraha *and* sarvodaya, *arguing that no one can be free until all are free, that liberty must imply equality, and that the only method for achieving this is through nonviolence.*

His difference with socialists and communists concerned the use of violence. As the first article in this section, entitled "Answers to Zamindars," states: "I shall throw the whole weight of my influence in preventing class war." Gandhi wanted a social and economic revolution to ensure the welfare of all, but he would not sanction violence in any form to achieve it. He appealed, therefore, to landlords to act as "trustees" of their wealth by permitting its public use. If capitalists develop a stronger social conscience and civic sense, then gross disparity of wealth might give way to a gradual transformation into an egalitarian society. As he says in one of the articles that follows, his "doctrine of trusteeship" met with ridicule, but he adhered to it as the only alternative to a violent revolution.

He repeatedly makes "economic independence" a part of sarvodaya. *By this he means that an individual or a nation must be self-reliant, imbued with a spirit of self-discipline and industry. "Welfare of all" denoted economic justice and equal opportunity, not dependency or the welfare system as we know it in America. The staunch self-reliance found in his economics is evident in the interview included here regarding U.S. aid to India, where he says, "There is nothing more degrading for a country than to beg from others when it cannot meet its requirements." Then he characteristically concludes by arguing from the personal to the international: "It is a practical principle that if you want to be friends with someone and if you want the friendship to endure, you should not seek economic aid from them. So, however rich America may be we shall only become crippled if we seek economic aid from her." Gandhi's idealism is usually associated with compassion and charity, but*

*in his appeal to discipline and hard work there is an undeniable strain of what
we might call "Yankee individualism." He identified with the gospel of self-
reliance in the philosophy of two of the Americans that he admired most,
Thoreau and Emerson.*

*Gandhi's economics seems particularly relevant today to our concerns about
the environment because of his insistence that we should not violate nature
through self-indulgence. In a plea for self-restraint, he distinguished between
essential needs and unnecessary accumulation of things, or between needs and
wants. His argument for disciplined voluntary control of the latter is the
magnetic center of all his thinking about economics. The concept of* sarvodaya
*is most optimistic when it asserts that people can summon the common sense to
exercise restraint in their own self-interest: not from an instinct of compassion
but born of a reasoned judgment that our planet cannot endure forever the
blight of endless acquisitiveness.*

ANSWERS TO ZAMINDARS

QUESTION: The Karachi Congress passed a resolution laying down the fundamental rights of the people and, since it recognized private property, nationalist
zamindars have supported the Congress. But the new Socialist Party in the Congress threatens the extinction of private property. How would it affect the Congress policy? Do you not think that this will precipitate class war? Will you
prevent it?

ANSWER: The Karachi resolution can be altered only by an open ses-
sion of the next Congress, but let me assure you that I shall be no party to
dispossessing the propertied classes of their private property without just
cause. My object is to reach your hearts and convert you so that you may
hold all your private property in trust for your tenants and use it primarily for their welfare.

I am aware of the fact that within the ranks of the Congress a new party
called the Socialist Party is coming into being [in 1934] and I cannot say
what would happen if that party succeeds in carrying the Congress with
it. But I am quite clear that if a strictly honest and unchallengeable refer-
endum of our millions were to be taken, they would not vote for wholesale
expropriation of the propertied classes. I am working for the co-operation
and co-ordination of capital and labor and of landlords and tenants. It is
open to you to join the Congress as much as it is open to the poorest by
paying the fee of four annas and subscribing to the Congress creed.

But I must utter a note of warning. I have always told the mill-owners
that they are not exclusive owners of the mills. Workmen are equal sharers

in the ownership. In the same way, I would tell you that the ownership of your land belongs as much to the ryots as to you and you may not squander your gains in luxurious or extravagant living, but must use them for the well being of the ryots. Once you make your ryots experience a sense of kinship with you and a sense of security that their interests as members of the family will never suffer at your hands, you may be sure that there cannot be a class war between you and them.

Class war is foreign to the essential genius of India which is capable of evolving a form of communism broad-based on the fundamental rights of all and equal justice to all. The *Ramarajya* of my dream ensures the rights alike of prince and pauper.

You may be sure that I shall throw the whole weight of my influence in preventing class war. . . .

Socialism and communism of the West are based on certain conceptions which are fundamentally different from ours. One such conception is their belief in the essential selfishness of human nature. I do not subscribe to it, for I know that the essential difference between man and brute is that the former can respond to the call of spirit in him and can rise superior to the passions that he owns in common with the brute and therefore superior to selfishness and violence which belong to brute nature and not to the immortal spirit of man.

That is the fundamental conception of Hinduism, which has years of penance and austerity at the back of the discovery of their truth. That is why whilst we had had saints who have burnt out their bodies and laid down their lives in order to explore the secrets of the soul, we have none as in the West who have laid down their lives in exploring the remotest or highest regions of earth. Our socialism or communism should therefore be based on non-violence and on the harmonious co-operation of labor and capital and the landlord and the tenant.[43]

ECONOMIC EQUALITY

This is the master-key to non-violent independence. Working for economic equality means abolishing the eternal conflict between capital and labor. It means the levelling down of the few rich in whose hands is concentrated the bulk of the nation's wealth on the one hand, and the levelling up of the semi-starved naked millions on the other. A non-violent system of government is clearly an impossibility so long as the wide gulf between the rich and the hungry millions persists. The contrast between the palaces of New Delhi and the miserable hovels of the poor laboring

class nearby cannot last one day in a free India in which the poor will enjoy the same power as the richest in the land. A violent and bloody revolution is a certainty one day unless there is a voluntary abdication of riches
and the power that riches give and sharing them for the common good.
I adhere to my doctrine of trusteeship in spite of the ridicule that
has been poured upon it. It is true that it is difficult to reach. So is non-
violence. But we made up our minds in 1920 to negotiate that steep as-
cent. We have found it worth the effort. It involves a daily growing appreciation of the working of non-violence. It is expected that Congressmen
will make a diligent search and reason out for themselves the why and the
wherefore of non-violence. They should ask themselves how the existing
inequalities can be abolished violently or non-violently. I think we know
the violent way. It has not succeeded anywhere. Some claim that it has in
Russia in a large measure. I doubt it. . . .
This non-violent experiment is still in the making. We have nothing
much yet to show by way of demonstration. It is certain, however, that the
method has begun to work though ever so slowly in the direction of equality. And since non-violence is a process of conversion, the conversion, if
achieved, must be permanent. A society or a nation constructed non-
violently must be able to withstand attack upon its structure from without
or within. We have moneyed Congressmen in the organization. They have
to lead the way. This fight provides an opportunity for the closest heart-
searching on the part of every individual Congressman. If ever we are to
achieve equality, the foundation has to be laid now. Those who think that
major reforms will come after the advent of swaraj are deceiving themselves as to the elementary working of non-violent swaraj. It will not drop
from heaven all of a sudden one fine morning. But it has to be built up
brick by brick by corporate self-effort. We have travelled a fair way in that
direction. But a much longer and weary distance has to be covered before we can behold swaraj in its glorious majesty. Every Congressman has
to ask himself what he has done towards the attainment of economic
equality.[44]
According to my definition, there cannot be true swaraj as long as there
is exploitation. Mere change from British to Indian rule does not mean
swaraj. As long as one class dominates over another, as long as the poor remain poor or become poorer, there will be no swaraj. In my swaraj the
millions will live happily. They will get good food, decent houses and
enough clothing. By good food I do not mean that they will eat sweets. But
everyone must get pure milk, pure ghee [butter] and sufficient fruit and
vegetables. I know I am talking tall because the poor today do not even

know what fruit is. During the mango season, they get a few mangoes and during the guava season they have a few guavas. They do not get any other fruit except these and a few others. They do not get even clean and nutritious foodgrain. They have to live on rotten rice, coarse grain and dirty salt. I wish everyone gets what they call a balanced diet as also a clean and comfortable house. This according to me is real freedom.[45]

INTERVIEW TO NIRMAL KUMAR BOSE

Q. Is love or non-violence compatible with possession or exploitation in any shape or form? If possession and non-violence cannot go together, then do you advocate the maintenance of private ownership of land or factories as an unavoidable evil which will continue so long as individuals are not ripe or educated enough to do without it? If it be such a step, would it not be better to own all the land through the State and place the State under the control of the masses?

A. Love and exclusive possession can never go together. Theoretically when there is perfect love, there must be perfect non-possession. The body is our last possession. So a man can only exercise perfect love and be completely dispossessed, if he is prepared to embrace death and renounce his body for the sake of human service.

But that is true in theory only. In actual life, we can hardly exercise perfect love, for the body as a possession will always remain with us. Man will ever remain imperfect, and it will always to be his part to try to be perfect. So that perfection in love or non-possession will remain an unattainable ideal, as long as we are alive, but towards which we must ceaselessly strive.

Those who own money now are asked to behave like trustees holding their riches on behalf of the poor. You may say that trusteeship is a legal fiction. But if people meditate over it constantly and try to act up to it, then life on earth would be governed far more by love than it is at present. Absolute trusteeship is an abstraction like Euclid's definition of a point, and is equally unattainable. But if we strive for it, we shall be able to go further in realizing a state of equality on earth than by any other method.

Q. If you say that private possession is incompatible with non-violence, why do you put up with it?

A. That is a concession one has to make to those who earn money but who would not voluntarily use their earnings for the benefit of mankind.

Q. Why then not have State-ownership in place of private property and thus minimize violence?

A. It is better than private ownership. But that too is objectionable on the ground of violence. It is my firm conviction that if the State suppressed capitalism by violence, it will be caught in the coils of violence itself, and will fail to develop non-violence at any time. The State represents violence in a concentrated and organized form. The individual has a soul, but as the State is a soulless machine, it can never be weaned from violence to which it owes its very existence. Hence I prefer the doctrine of trusteeship.

. . . I look upon an increase of the power of the State with the greatest fear, because although while apparently doing good by minimizing exploitation, it does the greatest harm to mankind by destroying individuality, which lies at the root of all progress. We know of so many cases where men have adopted trusteeship, but none where the State has really lived for the poor.[46]

Let there be no mistake about my conception of swaraj. It is complete independence of alien control and complete economic independence. So at one end you have political independence, at the other the economic. It has two other ends. One of them is moral and social, the corresponding end is dharma, i.e., religion in the highest sense of the term. It includes Hinduism, Islam, Christianity, etc., but is superior to them all. You may recognize it by the name of Truth, not the honesty of expedience but the living Truth that pervades everything and will survive all destruction and all transformation. Moral and social uplift may be recognized by the terms we are used to, i.e., non-violence. Let us call this the square of swaraj, which will be out of shape if any of its angles is untrue. In the language of the Congress we cannot achieve this political and economic freedom without truth and non-violence, in concrete terms without a living faith in God and hence moral and social elevation.

By political independence I do not mean an imitation of the British House of Commons, or the Soviet rule of Russia or the Fascist rule of Italy or the Nazi rule of Germany. . . . We must have ours suited to ours. . . . I have described it as *Ramarajya*, i.e., sovereignty of the people based on pure moral authority. . . .

Then take economic independence. It is not a product of industrialization of the modern or the Western type. Indian economic independence means to me the economic uplift of every individual, male and female, by his or her own conscious effort. Under that system all men and women will have enough clothing—not the mere loin-cloth, but what we understand by the term necessary articles of clothing and enough food including milk and butter which are today denied to millions.[47]

If America does not put her affluence to good use, its very affluence will ruin it. If America tries to win friendship of other countries with the help of her money, and if China, Japan, Iran, India, Pakistan or any other country gets involved with her even in a small degree, both will come to grief. That is why I have been daily telling Rajendra Babu* that import of foodgrains is the worst kind of slavery. There is nothing more degrading for a country than to beg from others when it cannot meet its requirements.

It is a practical principle that if you want to be friends with someone and if you want the friendship to endure, you should not seek economic aid from them. So, however rich America may be we shall only become crippled if we seek economic aid from her.[48]

SPEECH AT MEETING OF VILLAGE WORKERS, NAGPUR

I am afraid I must repeat the gospel to you and remind you that, when you demand swaraj, you do not want swaraj for yourself alone, but for your neighbor too. The principle is neither metaphysical nor too philosophical for comprehension. It is just good common sense. If you love thy neighbor as thyself, he will do likewise with you.

What you say about the difficulties of a worker in the villages is too true,† but we have got to falsify it. We have to be true villagers without their shortcomings and failings, and I am quite sure that, when we do so, there would be no difficulty for an honest laborer to earn a living wage. But let no one come and tell me: "I have a mother, three widowed sisters, a brother who has to be sent to England to be called to the Bar, another reading in Muir College and a third to be sent to the Indian Sandhurst." Sure enough, work in the villages will not give such a one a "living"! But it is possible to earn a genuine living for all the members of one's family, if all those members also will work, as do all the members in a peasant's family.

There is a conflict of interest between capital and labor, but we have to resolve it by doing our own duty. Just as pure blood is proof against poisonous germs, so will labor, when it is pure, be proof against exploitation. The laborer has but to realize that labor is also capital. As soon as laborers

*Dr. Rajendra Prasad, who became, in 1947, president of the Congress Party and first president of India.

†A worker had said that he had found it very difficult to live like a villager in a village and make ends meet.

are properly educated and organized and they realize their strength, no
amount of capital can subdue them. Organized and enlightened labor can
dictate its own terms. It is no use vowing vengeance against a party because we are weak. We have to get strong. Strong hearts, enlightened
minds and willing hands can brave all odds and remove all obstacles. No,
"Love thy neighbor as thyself" is no counsel of perfection. The capitalist
is as much a neighbor of the laborer as the latter is a neighbor of the former, and one has to seek and win the willing co-operation of the other.
Nor does the principle mean that we should accept exploitation lying
down. Our internal strength will render all exploitation impossible.[49]

The principles of economics are not, like the principles of mathematics,
for instance, immutable, and for all times and climes. England will not accept the economics of France, nor France that of Germany, nor Germany
that of America, and they would be wrong if they did so. A country which
produces no food-stuffs and produces only minerals must have different
economics from that which produces food-stuffs but has no mineral resources. India, therefore, cannot afford to go by the economics of France,
England, America or Germany. India was once the land of gold. Not that
it produced much gold, but it had such treasures of art, it produced cloth
of such rich quality and spices of such value that other lands paid for them
in treasures of gold. We have lost that proud position today and have become mere hewers of wood and drawers of water. But even now we can
regain that proud position, for, our natural resources are unique and no
other country in the world, excepting China, can boast of the crores of living machines we have. Now, how can a country with crores of living machines afford to have a machine which will displace the labor of crores of
living machines? It would spell their unemployment and their ruin. We
have to employ all these crores of human machines that are ideal, we have
to make them intelligent machines, and unless cities decide to depend for
the necessaries of life and for most of their other needs on the villages, this
can never happen. We are guilty of a grievous wrong against the villagers,
and the only way in which we can expedite it is by encouraging them to
revive their lost industries and arts by assuring them of a ready market.
There is no one more patient and forbearing than God, but there comes a
limit even to His patience and forbearance. If we neglect our duty to our
villagers, we shall be courting our own ruin. This duty is no onerous one.
It is incredibly simple. We have to be rural-minded and think of our
necessities and the necessities of our household in the terms of rural-
mindedness. The task does not involve much expenditure either. Volun-
teers are needed to go to the nearest village to assure them that all that

they produce would find a ready market in the towns and cities. This is a task which can be undertaken by men and women of all castes and creeds, of all parties and all faiths. It is in consonance with the true economics of our country.[50]

. . . I am not against machinery as such, but I am opposed to machinery that may be designed to displace the masses without giving them any adequate and satisfactory substitute.[51]

WHO IS A SOCIALIST?

Socialism is a beautiful word and so far as I am aware in socialism all the members of society are equal—none low, none high. In the individual body the head is not high because it is the top of the body, nor are the soles of the feet low because they touch the earth. Even as members of the individual body are equal so are the members of society. That is socialism.*

In it the prince and the peasant, the wealthy and the poor, the employer and the employee are all on the same level. In terms of religion there is no duality in socialism. It is all unity.

Looking at society all the world over there is nothing but duality or plurality. Unity is conspicuous by its absence. This man is high, that one is low, that one is a Hindu, that one a Muslim, third a Christian, fourth a Parsi, fifth a Sikh, sixth a Jew. Even among these there are sub-divisions. In the unity of my conception there is perfect unity in the plurality of designs.

In order to reach this state we may not look on things philosophically and say that we need not make a move until all are converted to socialism. Without changing our life we may go on giving addresses, forming parties and hawk-like seize the game when it comes our way. This is no socialism. The more we treat it as a game to be seized, the further it must recede from us.

Socialism begins with the first convert. If there is one such, you can add zeros to the one and the first zero will account for ten and every addition will account for ten times the previous number. If, however, the beginner is zero, in other words, no one makes the beginning, multiplicity of zeros will also produce zero value. Time and paper occupied in writing zeros will be so much waste.

*Gandhi was not a socialist. But some Indian nationalists were, and he was eager to include them in the independence movement. So he defines socialism here in ideal terms compatible with his own philosophy.

This socialism is as pure as crystal. It, therefore, requires crystal-like means to achieve it. Impure means result in an impure end. Hence the prince and the peasant will not be equalized by cutting off the prince's head, nor can the process of cutting off equalize the employer and the employee. One cannot reach truth by untruthfulness. Truthful conduct alone can reach truth. Are not non-violence and truth twins? The answer is an emphatic "no." Non-violence is embedded in truth and vice versa. Hence has it been said that they are faces of the same coin. Either is inseparable from the other. Read the coin either way. The spelling of words will be different. The value is the same. This blessed state is unattainable without perfect purity. Harbor impurity of mind or body and you have untruth and violence in you.

Therefore, only truthful, non-violent and pure-hearted socialists will be able to establish a socialistic society in India and the world. To my knowledge there is no country in the world which is purely socialistic. Without the means described above the existence of such a society is impossible.[52]

QUESTION: What exactly do you mean by economic equality? What is statutory trusteeship as conceived by you?

Gandhi's reply [paraphrased in the text] was that economic equality of his conception did not mean that everyone would literally have the same amount. It simply meant that everybody should have enough for his or her needs. . . . So the real meaning of economic equality was: "To each according to his needs." That was the definition of Marx. If a single man demanded as much as a man with wife and four children that would be a violation of economic equality. Gandhi continued:

Let no one try to justify the glaring difference between the classes and the masses, the prince and the pauper, by saying that the former need more. That will be ideal sophistry and a travesty of my argument. The contrast between the rich and the poor today is a painful sight. The poor villagers are exploited by the foreign Government and also by their own countrymen—the city-dwellers. They produce the food and go hungry. They produce milk and their children have to go without it. It is disgraceful. Everyone must have balanced diet, a decent house to live in, facilities for the education of one's children and adequate medical relief. . . .

Supposing India becomes a free country tomorrow, all the capitalists will have an opportunity of becoming statutory trustees. But such a statute will not be imposed from above. If will have to come from below. When the people understand the implications of trusteeship and the atmosphere is ripe for it, the people themselves, beginning with gram panchayats [village councils], will begin to introduce such statutes. Such a thing coming from below is easy to swallow. Coming from above, it is liable to prove a dead weight.

Q. What is the difference between your technique and that of the communists or socialists for realizing the goal of economic equality?

A. The socialists and communists say, they can do nothing to bring about economic equality today. They will just carry on propaganda in its favor and to that end they believe in generating and accentuating hatred. They say, when they get control over the State, they will enforce equality. Under my plan the State will be there to carry out the will of the people, not to dictate to them or force them to do its will. I shall bring about economic equality through non-violence, by converting the people to my point of view by harnessing the forces of love as against hatred. I will not wait till I have converted the whole society to my view but will straightaway make a beginning with myself. It goes without saying that I cannot hope to bring about economic equality of my conception, if I am the owner of fifty motor-cars or even of ten bighas of land. For that I have to reduce myself to the level of the poorest of the poor. That is what I have been trying to do for the last fifty years or more, and so I claim to be a foremost communist although I make use of cars and other facilities offered to me by the rich. They have no hold on me and I can shed them at a moment's notice, if the interests of the masses demand it.

Q. What is the place of satyagraha in making the rich realize their duty towards the poor?

A. The same as against the foreign power. Satyagraha is a law of universal application. Beginning with the family, its use can be extended to every other circle. Supposing a land-owner exploits his tenants and mulcts them of the fruit of their toil by appropriating it to his own use. When they expostulate with him, he does not listen and raises objections that he requires so much for his wife, so much for his children and so on. The tenants or those who have espoused their cause and have influence, will make an appeal to his wife to expostulate with her husband. She would probably say that for herself she does not need his exploited money. The children will say likewise that they would earn for themselves what they need.

Supposing further that he listens to nobody or that his wife and children combine against the tenants, they will not submit. They will quit, if asked to do so, but they will make it clear that the land belongs to him who tills it. The owner cannot till all the land himself, and he will have to give in to their just demands. It may, however, be that the tenants are replaced by others. Agitation short of violence will then continue till the replaced tenants see their error and make common cause with the evicted tenants. Thus satyagraha is a process of educating public opinion such that it covers all the elements of society and in the end makes itself irresistible. Violence interrupts the process and prolongs the real revolution of the whole social structure.[53]

Sustained public education is what is wanted. Conversion is our motto, not coercion. Coercion is an offspring of violence. Conversion is a fruit of non-violence and love.

The question is, if you will benefit the workers, the peasant and the factory hand, can you avoid class war?

I can, most decidedly, if only the people will follow the non-violent method. The past twelve months have abundantly shown the possibilities of non-violence adopted even as a policy. When the people adopt it as a principle of conduct, class war becomes an impossibility. The experiment in that direction is being tried in Ahmedabad. It has yielded most satisfactory results and there is every likelihood of its proving conclusive. By the non-violent method we seek not to destroy the capitalist, we seek to destroy capitalism. We invite the capitalist to regard himself as trustee for those on whom he depends for the making, the retention and the increase of his capital. Nor need the worker wait for his conversion. If capital is power, so is work. Either power can be used destructively or creatively. Either is dependent on the other. Immediately the worker realizes his strength, he is in a position to become a co-sharer with the capitalist instead of remaining his slave. If he aims at becoming the sole owner, he will most likely be killing the hen that lays golden eggs. Inequalities in intelligence and even opportunity will last till the end of time. A man living on the banks of a river has any day more opportunity of growing crops than one living in an arid desert. But if inequalities stare us in the face the essential equality too is not to be missed. Every man has an equal right to the necessaries of life even as birds and beasts have. And since every right carries with it a corresponding duty and the corresponding remedy for resisting any attack upon it, it is merely a matter of finding out the corresponding duties and remedies to vindicate the elementary fundamental equality. The corresponding duty is to labour with my limbs and the corresponding remedy is to non-cooperate with him who deprives me of the fruit of my labour. And if I would recognize the fundamental equality, as I must, of the capitalist and the labourer, I must not aim at his destruction. I must strive for his conversion. My non-co-operation with him will open his eyes to the wrong he may be doing. Nor need I be afraid of someone else taking my place when I have non-co-operated. For I expect to influence my co-workers so as not to help the wrongdoing of employer. This kind of education of the mass of workers is no doubt a slow process, but as it is also the surest, it is necessarily the quickest. It can be easily demonstrated that destruction of the capitalist must mean destruction in the end of the worker and as no human being is so bad as to be beyond redemption, no human being is so perfect as to warrant his destroying him whom he wrongly considers to be wholly evil.[54]

THE REALITIES

The Congress must progressively represent the masses. They are as yet untouched by politics. They have no political consciousness of the type our politicians desire. Their politics are confined to bread and salt—I dare not say butter, for millions do not know the taste of ghee or even oil. Their politics are confined to communal adjustments. It is right however to say that we the politicians do represent the masses in opposition to the Government. But if we begin to use them before they are ready, we shall cease to represent them. We must first come in living touch with them by working for them and in their midst. We must share their sorrows, understand their difficulties and anticipate their wants. With the pariahs we must be pariahs and see how we feel to clean the closets [toilets] of the upper classes and have the remains of their table thrown at us. We must see how we like being in the boxes, miscalled houses, of the laborers of Bombay. We must identify ourselves with the villagers who toil under the hot sun beating on their bent backs and see how we would like to drink water from the pool in which the villagers bathe, wash their clothes and pots and in which their cattle drink and roll. Then and not till then shall we truly represent the masses and they will, as surely as I am writing this, respond to every call.

"We cannot all do this, and if we are to do this, good-bye to swaraj for a thousand years and more," some will say. I shall sympathize with the objection. But I do claim that some of us at least will have to go through the agony and out of it only will a nation full, vigorous and free be born. I suggest to all that they should give their mental co-operation and that they should mentally identify themselves with the masses.[55]

Gandhi was an activist who believed fervently in the power of ideas. He declared that "the true movement consists in revolutionizing ideas. Action always follows ideas."[56] His originality, especially in his theories of satyagraha

and swaraj, *has been highlighted throughout this collection. Yet he also reinforced old concepts, none more important than his idea of democracy, an idea
new to India but one that Gandhi unhesitatingly took from western political
philosophy and applied to his own freedom struggle. If action ever followed an
idea, then India provides a classic case: it became, with the force of Gandhi's
leadership, the world's largest democracy.*

*In some respects, Gandhi's theory of democracy relies completely on
western political thought, such as his emphasis on civil rights and liberties
found in his "Resolution on Fundamental Rights." He consistently related
liberty to democracy, as in his statement that "freedom of speech and corresponding action is the breath of democratic life."*[57] *The first entry in this
section opens with his definition of democracy as "the rule of the people, by
the people, for the people," straight from Lincoln.*

*But Gandhi also infuses his own thinking into the idea of democracy. In
this same article he equates "true democracy" with "swaraj," which must
come through "unadulterated* ahimsa*" or nonviolence. Equally distinctive, he
identified democracy with his favorite virtues of discipline and restraint: "A
born democrat is a born disciplinarian," with a "willing submission to social
restraint." These ideas are not characteristic of the western democratic tradition; Gandhi has developed them from his own political context.*

DUTY, DEMOCRACY AND SWARAJ

You want democracy—the rule of the people, by the people, for the people. Surely, all the 75,000 people of Rajkot* cannot become rulers or administrators. Democracy must in essence, therefore, mean the art and science of mobilizing the entire physical, economic and spiritual resources
of all the various sections of the people in the service of the common good
of all.

Service of the family has been the motive behind all our activities hitherto. We must now learn to broaden our outlook so as to include in our
ambit the service of the people as a whole.

We are familiar with several conceptions of village work. Hitherto it has
mostly meant propaganda in the villages to inculcate upon the village
masses a sense of their rights. Sometimes it has also meant conducting
welfare activity among them to ameliorate their material condition. But
the village work that I have now come to place before you consists in educating the villager in his duties.

*City in the western state of Gujarat.

Rights accrue automatically to him who duly performs his duties. In fact the right to perform one's duties is the only right that is worth living for and dying for. It covers all legitimate rights. All the rest is garb under one guise or another and contains in it seeds of *himsa*.

The swaraj of my conception will come only when all of us are firmly persuaded that our swaraj has got to be won, worked and maintained through truth and ahimsa alone. True democracy or the swaraj of the masses can never come through untruthful and violent means, for the simple reason that the natural corollary to their use would be to remove all opposition through the suppression or extermination of the antagonists. That does not make for individual freedom. Individual freedom can have the fullest play only under a regime of unadulterated ahimsa.

We cannot afford to have discord in our midst if we are to educate the people. We must all speak with one voice. If we want to weld the various sections into one people—and that is the *sine qua non* of democracy—we may not, in rendering service, make any distinction between those who took part in our struggle and those who did not.[58]

We want to set up democracy in Rajkot. A born democrat is a born disciplinarian. Democracy comes naturally to him who is habituated normally to yield willing obedience to all laws, human or divine. I claim to be a democrat both by instinct and training. Let those who are ambitious to serve democracy qualify themselves by satisfying first this acid test of democracy. Moreover, a democrat must be utterly selfless. He must think and dream not in terms of self or party but only of democracy. Only then does he acquire the right of civil disobedience. I do not want anybody to give up his convictions or to suppress himself. I do not believe that a healthy and honest difference of opinion will injure our cause. But opportunism, camouflage or patched-up compromises certainly will. If you must dissent, you should take care that your opinions voice your innermost convictions and are not intended merely as a convenient party cry.

Today our democracy is choked by our internecine strife. We are torn by dissensions—dissensions between Hindus and Mussalmans, Brahmins and non-Brahmins, Congressmen and non-Congressmen. It is no easy task to evolve democracy out of this mobocracy. Let us not make confusion worse confounded by further introducing into it the virus of sectionalism and party spirit.

I value individual freedom but you must not forget that man is essentially a social being. He has risen to this present status by learning to adjust his individualism to the requirements of social progress. Unrestricted individualism is the law of the beast of the jungle. We have learnt to strike

the mean between individual freedom and social restraint. Willing submission to social restraint for the sake of the well-being of the whole society enriches both the individual and the society of which one is a member.[59]
Democracy disciplined and enlightened is the finest thing in the world.
A democracy prejudiced, ignorant, superstitious will land itself in chaos
and may be self-destroyed.[60]

I hold that self-government is not an end, but only a means to good
government. And true democracy is what promotes the welfare of the
people. The test of a good government lies in the largest good of the people with the minimum of controls. The test of autocracy, socialism, capitalism, etc., is also people's welfare or good government. In themselves
they are of no value. Any system of government can fail if people do not
have honesty and a feeling of brotherhood. There may be work, there may
be women to do the work and tools with which to do it, yet in my view a
system that admits of poverty and unemployment is not fit to survive even
for a day.[61]

Democracy is where even the man in the street is heard. When we are
out to establish a democratic order, the Viceroy's House, or even Jawaharlal's [Nehru] house, is not the seat of the Government. I have described
Jawaharlal as the uncrowned king. And we are a poor nation. We are so
poor that we shall walk rather than ride in a car. Even if somebody offers
us a lift in his car, we shall decline his offer saying that he can keep his car,
we would rather walk. If we are over-hungry, we shall eat a little more.
Thus democracy means the rule of the man in the street.[62]

Democracy is an impossible thing until the power is shared by all, but
let not democracy degenerate into mobocracy. Even a pariah, a laborer,
who makes it possible for you to earn your living, will have his share in
self-government. But you will have to touch their lives. Go to them, see
their hovels where they live packed like sardines. It is up to you to look
after this part of humanity. It is possible for you to make their lives or mar
their lives.[63]

In this age of democracy it is essential that desired results are achieved
by the collective effort of the people. It will no doubt be good to achieve
an objective through the effort of a supremely powerful individual, but
it can never make the community conscious of its corporate strength. An
individual's success will be like a millionaire doling free food to millions
of starving people. We should, therefore, bend our energies to a fulfillment of the thirteenfold constructive programme. It may or may not
bring swaraj, but we shall surely have the satisfaction of having done
our best.[64]

All Hindus, Muslims, Sikhs, Parsis, Christians and Jews who people this country from Kanyakumari to Kashmir and from Karachi to Dibrugarh in Assam and who have lovingly and in a spirit of service adopted it as their dear motherland, have an equal right to it. No one can say that it has place only for the majority and the minority should be dishonored. Whoever serves it with the purest devotion must have the first right over it. Therefore, anyone who seeks to drive out the Muslims is Delhi's enemy number one and therefore India's enemy number one. We are heading towards that catastrophe. Every Indian must do his bit to ward it off.

What should we do then? If we would see Panchayat Raj, i.e., democracy established, we would regard the humblest and the lowliest Indian as being equally the ruler of India with the tallest in the land. For this everyone should be pure. If they are not they should become so. He who is pure will also be wise. He will observe no distinctions between caste and caste, between touchable and untouchable, but will consider everyone equal with himself. He will bind others to himself with love. To him no one would be an untouchable. He would treat the laborers the same as he would the capitalists. He will, like the millions of toilers, earn his living from service of others and will make no distinction between intellectual and manual work. To hasten this desirable consummation, we should voluntarily turn ourselves into scavengers. He who is wise will never touch opium, liquor or any intoxicants. He will observe the vow of swadeshi and regard every woman who is not his wife as his mother, sister or daughter according to her age, and never see anyone with eyes of lust. He will concede to woman the same rights he claims for himself. If need be he will sacrifice his own life but never kill another.[65]

. . . I have suggested that you [a Hindu majority, in 1947, after independence] should adopt the ways followed by all democratic countries. In democracy, every individual has to abide by the wishes of the people, that is, the Government, and has to direct his own wishes in that light. If every man takes the law into his own hands the State cannot function. It would mean anarchy, which means end of social order. That is, the State would not exist. That is the way to lose our independence. I believe that if you would let the Government carry out its tasks, there is no doubt that every Hindu and Sikh refugee would return home with honor and respect. But you cannot expect these things to happen if you want your Muslim compatriots to be driven out of India. I find any such thing dreadful. You cannot secure justice by doing injustice to the Muslims.[66]

The spirit of democracy, which is fast spreading throughout India and the rest of the world, will, without a shadow of doubt, purge the institution of the idea of predominance and subordination. The spirit of democracy is not a mechanical thing to be adjusted by abolition of forms. It requires change of the heart. If caste is a bar to the spread of that spirit, the existence of five religions in India—Hinduism, Islam, Christianity, Zoroastrianism, and Judaism—is equally a bar. The spirit of democracy requires the inculcation of the spirit of brotherhood, and I can find no difficulty in considering a Christian or a Mohammedan to be my brother in absolutely the same sense as a blood brother, and Hinduism that is responsible for the doctrine of caste is also responsible for the inculcation of the essential brotherhood, not merely of man but even of all that lives.[67]

DEMOCRACY AND NON-VIOLENCE

Q. Why do you say, "Democracy can only be saved through non-violence?"

A. Because democracy, so long as it is sustained by violence, cannot provide for or protect the weak. My notion of democracy is that under it the weakest should have the same opportunity as the strongest. That can never happen except through non-violence. No country in the world today shows any but patronizing regard for the weak. The weakest, you say, go to the wall. Take your own case [the questioner was an American]. Your land is owned by a few capitalist owners. The same is true of South Africa. These large holdings cannot be sustained except by violence, veiled if not open. Western democracy, as it functions today, is diluted Nazism or Fascism. At best it is merely a cloak to hide the Nazi and the Fascist tendencies of imperialism. Why is there the war today, if it is not for the satisfaction of the desire to share the spoils? It was not through democratic methods that Britain bagged India. What is the meaning of South African democracy? Its very constitution has been drawn to protect the white man against the colored man, the natural occupant. Your own history is perhaps blacker still, in spite of what the Northern States did for the abolition of slavery. The way you have treated the Negro presents a discreditable record. And it is to save such democracies that the war is being fought! There is something very hypocritical about it. I am thinking just now in terms of non-violence and trying to expose violence in its nakedness.

India is trying to evolve true democracy, i.e., without violence. Our weapons are those of satyagraha expressed through the charkha, the village industries, primary education through handicrafts, removal of untouchability, communal harmony, prohibition, and non-violent organization of labor as in Ahmedabad. These mean mass effort and mass education. We have big agencies for conducting these activities. They are purely voluntary, and their only sanction is service of the lowliest.

This is the permanent part of the non-violent effort. From this effort is created the capacity to offer non-violent resistance called non-co-operation and civil disobedience which may culminate in mass refusal to pay rent and taxes. As you know, we have tried non-co-operation and civil disobedience on a fairly large scale and fairly successfully. The experiment has in it promise of a brilliant future. As yet our resistance has been that of the weak. The aim is to develop the resistance of the strong. Your wars will never ensure safety for democracy. India's experiment can and will, if the people come up to the mark or, to put it another way, if God gives me the necessary wisdom and strength to bring the experiment to fruition.[68]

One thing is certain. If the mad race for armaments continues, it is bound to result in a slaughter such as has never occurred in history. If there is a victor left the very victory will be a living death for the nation that emerges victorious. There is no escape from the impending doom save through a bold and unconditional acceptance of the non-violent method with all its glorious implications. Democracy and violence can ill go together. The States that are today nominally democratic have either to become frankly totalitarian or, if they are to become truly democratic, they must become courageously non-violent. It is a blasphemy to say that non-violence can only be practiced by individuals and never by nations which are composed of individuals.[69]

Q. Would you kindly give a broad but comprehensive picture of the Independent India of your own conception?

Independence must begin at the bottom. Thus, every village will be a republic or panchayat having full powers. It follows, therefore, that every village has to be self-sustained and capable of managing its affairs even to the extent of defending itself against the whole world. It will be trained and prepared to perish in the attempt to defend itself against any on-slaught from without. Thus, ultimately, it is the individual who is the unit. This does not exclude dependence on and willing help from neighbors or from the world. It will be free and voluntary play of mutual forces. Such a society is necessarily highly cultured in which every man and woman knows what he or she wants and, what is more, knows that no one should want anything that others cannot have with equal labor.

This society must naturally be based on truth and non-violence which, in my opinion, are not possible without a living belief in God, meaning a self-existent, all-knowing living Force which inheres every other force known to the world and which depends on none and which will live when all other forces may conceivably perish or cease to act. I am unable to account for my life without belief in this all-embracing living light.

In this structure composed of innumerable villages, there will be ever-widening, never-ascending circles. Life will not be a pyramid with the apex sustained by the bottom. But it will be an oceanic circle whose center will be the individual always ready to perish for the village, the latter ready to perish for the circle of villages, till at last the whole becomes one life composed of individuals, never aggressive in their arrogance but ever humble, sharing the majesty of the oceanic circle of which they are integral units.

Therefore the outermost circumference will not wield power to crush the inner circle but will give strength to all within and derive its own strength from it. I may be taunted with the retort that this is all Utopian and, therefore, not worth a single thought. If Euclid's point, though incapable of being drawn by human agency, has an imperishable value, my picture has its own for mankind to live. Let India live for this true picture, though never realizable in its completeness. We must have a proper picture of what we want, before we can have something approaching it. If there ever is to be a republic of every village in India, then I claim verity for my picture in which the last is equal to the first or, in other words, no one is to be the first and none the last.

In this picture every religion has its full and equal place. We are all leaves of a majestic tree whose trunk cannot be shaken off its roots which are deep down in the bowels of the earth. The mightiest wind cannot move it.

In this there is no room for machines that would displace human labor and that would concentrate power in a few hands. Labor has its unique place in a cultured human family. Every machine that helps every individual has a place.[70]

The metaphor of the "oceanic circle" where, beginning with the individual, each entity sacrifices itself for the good of the larger unit, should not disguise the importance of the person in Gandhi's thought. For all of its attention to forms of social organization, Hinduism is profoundly individualistic in the sense of recognizing, above all, the sanctity of self-realization. Gandhi followed this emphasis in his thought. In a reply to a letter from a nephew, he discussed in detail personal questions concerning "the cause of our bondage as well as of our freedom," and then concluded with this wisdom: "I hope I have replied to all your questions. Please do not carry unnecessarily on your head the burden of emancipating India. Emancipate your own self. Even that burden is very great. Apply everything to yourself. Nobility of soul consists in realizing that you are yourself India. In your emancipation is the emancipation of India." [71]

Notes to Part II

1. *CWMG* 10: 64. *Hind Swaraj*, November 22, 1909.
2. Ashis Nandy, *The Intimate Enemy: Loss and Recovery of Self under Colonialism* (Delhi: Oxford University Press, 1983), 63.
3. *CWMG* 38: 1–2. November 1, 1928.
4. Ibid., 18. November 4, 1928.
5. *CWMG* 27: 134. May 21, 1925.
6. *CWMG* 35: 456–57. January 12, 1928.
7. *CWMG* 21: 458. November 17, 1921.
8. *CWMG* 35: 294. December 1, 1927.
9. *CWMG* 37: 250–51. September 9, 1928.
10. *CWMG* 73: 22. September 16, 1940.
11. *CWMG* 45: 370–71. March 31, 1931.
12. Ibid., 372–74. March 31, 1931.
13. *CWMG* 46: 166–67. May 28, 1931.
14. *CWMG* 47: 235–36. July 30, 1931.
15. *CWMG* 22: 176–78. January 12, 1922.
16. *CWMG* 69: 52. March 13, 1939.
17. *CWMG* 38: 18. November 4, 1928.
18. *CWMG* 72: 378–81. August 18, 1940.
19. *CWMG* 10: 28–32. *Hind Swaraj* (1909).
20. *CWMG* 42: 380–81. January 9, 1930.
21. *CWMG* 24: 139–40. May 29, 1924.
22. *CWMG* 24: 153. May 25, 1924.
23. *CWMG* 20: 436–38. July 28, 1921.
24. *CWMG* 19: 538–41. April 7, 1921.
25. *CWMG* 26: 52. January 29, 1925.
26. *CWMG* 21: 320. October 20, 1921.
27. *CWMG* 35: 461. January 15, 1928.
28. *CWMG* 55: 352. August 12, 1933.
29. *CWMG* 50: 369. August 14, 1932.
30. *CWMG* 19: 242–43. January 19, 1921.
31. *CWMG* 24: 227. June 12, 1924.
32. *CWMG* 47: 246–47. August 2, 1931.

33. *CWMG* 54: 416–17. April 15, 1933.
34. *CWMG* 57: 146–48. February 16, 1934.
35. *CWMG* 56: 215–16. November 11, 1933.
36. *CWMG* 62: 121–22. November 16, 1935.
37. *CWMG* 75: 149. December 13, 1941.
38. *CWMG* 6: 283. January 19, 1907.
39. *CWMG* 64: 165. December 24, 1936.
40. *CWMG* 33: 148–49. March 10, 1927.
41. *CWMG* 14: 202–6. February 20, 1918.
42. *CWMG* 22: 181–82. January 15, 1922.
43. *CWMG* 58: 274–78. July 25, 1934.
44. *CWMG* 75: 158–59. December 13, 1941.
45. *CWMG* 75: 6–7. October 12, 1941.
46. *CWMG* 59: 316–19. November 9, 1934.
47. *CWMG* 64: 191–92. December 27, 1936.
48. *CWMG* 88: 365. July 18, 1947.
49. *CWMG* 60: 254–55. February 23, 1935.
50. *CWMG* 60: 255–56. February 23, 1935.
51. *CWMG* 36: 446. June 21, 1928.
52. *CWMG* 88: 282–83. July 6, 1947.
53. *CWMG* 83: 26–28. January 24, 1946.
54. *CWMG* 45: 339–40. March 26, 1931.
55. *CWMG* 25: 121–22. September 11, 1924.
56. *CWMG* 25: 446. December 21, 1924.
57. *CWMG* 73: 34. September 22, 1940.
58. *CWMG* 69: 50. May 20, 1939.
59. *CWMG* 69: 258. May 27, 1939.
60. *CWMG* 47: 236. July 30, 1931.
61. *CWMG* 90: 325. December 30, 1947.
62. *CWMG* 88: 67. June 3, 1947.
63. *CWMG* 35: 298. December 1, 1927.
64. *CWMG* 72: 437. September 2, 1940.
65. *CWMG* 90: 419–20. January 14, 1948.
66. *CWMG* 89: 196. September 17, 1947.
67. *CWMG* 19: 84. August 12, 1920.
68. *CWMG* 72: 60–61. May 18, 1940.
69. *CWMG* 68: 94–95. November 5, 1938.
70. *CWMG* 85: 32–33. July 28, 1946.
71. *CWMG* 10: 206–7. April 2, 1910.

Chronology

1869   October 2: Mohandas Karamchand Gandhi, son of Karamchand and Putlibai Gandhi, born in Porbandar (population 72,000) on the western coast of India. The family was of the vaisya caste.

1876–1887   Educated at primary school and Alfred High School in Rajkot (pop. 37,000).

1882   Marries Kasturbai Makanji, both age thirteen.

1888   Birth of Harilal, the first of four children, all sons. The others are Manilal (1892), Ramdas (1897), and Devadas (1900).

1888–1891   Studies law at the Inner Temple in London. In June 1891, called to the Bar, then returns to India.

1893   Fails to practice law successfully at home; sails to South Africa as legal aid to an Indian company. Experiences brutal racial prejudice on the train to Pretoria and resolves to combat it.

1894   Establishes the Natal Indian Congress to oppose discriminatory legislation against the Indian community in South Africa.

1899   Organizes Indian Ambulance Corps and serves in the Boer War with the English colonial government.

1904   After establishing a successful law practice in South Africa, founds the Phoenix Settlement near Durban and begins experiments in simple living.

1906   Organizes an Ambulance Corps to assist British government against the "Zulu rebellion." Bitterly disillusioned by English brutality in the war. In July he takes vow of chastity (*brahmacharya*) to gain greater self-discipline. At September meeting of Indians in Johannesburg, he calls for civil disobedience against repressive government legislation. Later he recalls this moment as the "advent of *satyagraha*" or of militant nonviolent action.

1908   Arrested and imprisoned in January and again in October to December for civil disobedience.

1909   After three months in prison, sails for London to consult with friends. On the return journey in November, writes his first important treatise, entitled *Hind Swaraj* ("Indian Independence"). Translates Leo Tolstoy's "Letter to a Hindoo."

1910   Establishes a second settlement in South Africa, "Tolstoy Farm," to train and accommodate Indian civil resisters.

1913   Leads march of over two thousand Indian coal miners and workers on sugar plantations—men, women, and children—to protest discriminatory legislation and abusive work conditions. March lasts from November 6 to 10, after which Gandhi is arrested and imprisoned for a month.

1914   In January, Gandhi negotiates terms favorable to the Indian community with General Jan Smuts, leader of the South African government. In July, sails first to England, and then, in December, to India.

1917   Organizes and leads his first *satyagraha* or nonviolent protest in India, mobilizing sharecroppers to protest unjust labor conditions in Champaran, a district in a remote northern part of the country.

1918   Fasts to resolve a dispute between millowners and millworkers in Ahmedabad.

1919   Oppressive legislation by the British government in India prompts Gandhi to organize the first nation-wide *satyagraha* campaign. The government responds with repression and martial law that culminates in a massacre of four hundred Indians in the city of Amritsar, northern India, on April 13. This event has a profound effect on Gandhi, turning him into a full-fledged revolutionary, although firmly committed to nonviolence.

1921   After extensive mobilization of the people through the Indian National Congress organization, Gandhi proclaims the beginning of mass civil disobedience in December, with a national campaign of nonviolent non-cooperation.

1922   After violence breaks out among Indians, and police are killed in the town of Chauri Chaura, Gandhi calls off the campaign in February, and on March 10 he is arrested and sentenced to six years' imprisonment; he is released, however, in 1924, after having surgery in prison.

1928–29   A campaign of tax resistance among peasants in the region of Bardoli, western India, is so successful locally that it inspires Gandhi to plan another national civil-disobedience movement. In December 1929, the annual meeting of the Indian National Congress in the city of Lahore empowers Gandhi to inaugurate the next all-India campaign in the coming year.

1930   Begins the most energetic political movement of his life. On March 12 he leaves his ashram in Ahmedabad to march with eighty of his followers over two hundred miles to the shores of western India. There, near the village of Dandi, on April 6, he defies the government's tax on salt by collecting natural salt deposits. The action is symbolic but it mobilizes millions of Indians to break the law by following his example and on May 5 he is arrested and imprisoned.

1931   Released on January 26 to negotiate a settlement with the British Viceroy, Lord Irwin. Attends a Round Table Conference in London from September 12 to December 5.

1932   Returns to India and is arrested again on January 4 as negotiations for independence prove fruitless and another campaign seems likely. While in prison, he fasts from September 20 to 24 to protest the government policy toward untouchability.

1933   Released on May 8, arrested again on August 1, and, after he fasts on August 16, released again. Government unable to handle the threat of more civil disobedience, yet cannot justify permanent imprisonment of Gandhi.

1934–39   Concentrates on his social reform "Constructive Program" consisting of Hindu-Muslim unity, abolition of untouchability, and economic uplift of the villages through revival of craft industries such as *khadi* (homespun cotton cloth) production.

1940   Limited civil disobedience movement is launched on October 17.

1942   Begins last national civil-disobedience movement as he proposes "Quit India" resolution to the Indian Congress on August 8; millions respond to this call for the British to leave India and the government repression is harsh. Arrested and imprisoned on August 9.

1944   Kasturbai dies on February 22 while imprisoned with Gandhi; he is released on May 6. By this time, the Muslim League, under the leadership of M. A. Jinnah, has mobilized the Muslim majority areas behind its demand for a separate nation of Pakistan and Gandhi begins talks with Jinnah on September 9.

1946   India is plunged into civil war on August 16 when mass violence erupts in Calcutta between Hindus and Muslims over the demand for Pakistan. In four days of riots, four thousand are killed and eleven thousand injured. Communal (religious) violence spreads through Bengal and Gandhi responds by trying to calm its villages, walking 116 miles through the remote area of Noakhali in November–December.

1947   India attains independence on August 15 but it is partitioned as Pakistan emerges as the nation of Islam. As the civil war intensifies, Gandhi goes to Calcutta. This time he fasts, from September 1 to 4, for Hindu–Muslim unity. His success comes as the city becomes peaceful for the first time in a year and "the miracle of Calcutta" is proclaimed as one of his greatest feats of nonviolent action.

1948   Gandhi fasts in New Delhi to overcome communal violence there, from January 13 to 18. He declares: "I do not wish to live if peace is not established in India and Pakistan." On January 30, he is assassinated by a Hindu fanatic, Nathuram Vinayak Godse, motivated by Gandhi's tolerance of Muslims.

Glossary

Abhaya: Fearlessness. A vital component of Gandhi's thought because he stressed courage as an indispensable element of *satyagraha*.

Ahimsa: Nonviolence, conceived as both a personal and a political value as an active agent of change.

Ashram: Spiritual community. Gandhi established ashrams in Sabarmati (near Ahmedabad) in Gujarat and in Sevagram (near Wardha) in Maharashtra.

Atman: The universal self.

Bania: Subcaste to which Gandhi belonged within the vaishya social order in the system of four *varnas*.

Bapu: "Father," a general term of affection and respect often applied to Gandhi as father of the nation.

Bhagavad-Gita (often shortened to *Gita*): A philosophical dialogue and sacred text of Hinduism that had a profound influence on Gandhi.

Brahmacharya: Vow of celibacy. Taken by Gandhi in 1906 to signify devotion to God, self-discipline, and commitment to public service.

Charka: Spinning wheel, promoted by Gandhi in his effort to spread the use of Khadi.

Communalism: Conflict and intolerance among religious communities of Hindus, Muslims, and Sikhs.

Daridranarayan: "Divinity of the poor," a term used by Gandhi and others to support social change.

Darshan: A sight or view of holiness that conveys a blessing, adapted by Gandhi to mean that Indians must have the *darshan* of the "goddess of swaraj."

Dharma: Religion and religious duty; adherence to the Hindu code of morality. Its opposite is *adharma* or immorality.

Duragraha: Biased action by an individual or group to attain a selfish goal. Although an act of *duragraha* may not commit physical violence, it will harbor "violence of the spirit" in the form of anger and enmity.

Gandhi also called this "passive resistance," and distinguished it from *satyagraha*.

Dyerism: Signifies the brutal abuse of power seen in British imperialism, derived from Gen. Reginald Dyer, commander of troops responsible for the massacre of four hundred Indians at Amritsar in 1919.

Goonda: Thug or street criminal; the English word "goon" derives from it. In Calcutta, during partition, goondas terrorized both Hindus and Muslims, thus contributing to an epidemic of urban and communal violence. "Goondaism" signified a kind of social disease sanctioned by a city consumed with fear and conflict.

Harijan: "Child of God," Gandhi's term for a member of the untouchable community. Also the title of his weekly journal after 1933.

Hartal: Mass strike by labor and business as an act of *satyagraha* and nonviolent noncooperation against British rule.

Hind Swaraj: "Indian Home Rule," the title of Gandhi's first book, published in 1909 in South Africa and setting forth the basis of his political thought, especially the connection between *swaraj* and *satyagraha*.

Karmayoga: "Discipline (yoga) of action" set forth in the *Bhagavad-Gita*. Gandhi interpreted it as a gospel of political and social action, performed in a selfless manner, without desire for personal rewards.

Khadi: Homespun cotton cloth. Gandhi urged its production (by the spinning wheel) and use as the dress of the nationalist movement to symbolize identification with the masses and practice of *swadeshi*. Also called *khaddar*.

Mahatma: "Great [Maha] Soul [Atma]." An honorific title bestowed on Gandhi by Rabindranath Tagore.

Moksha: Spiritual liberation. Gandhi sometimes interpreted this as synonymous with *swaraj*, but *moksha* usually did not connote political independence.

Panchayat: Village council; local organ of political administration advocated by Gandhi to form the basic unit of a decentralized system of democracy in an independent India.

Partition: Political division of British India into two independent nations, India and Pakistan, in August 1947. Gandhi opposed the plan of partition but ultimately yielded to it in the face of civil war.

Raj: Government, denoting in Gandhi's period the administrative system of British rule over its colony, India. The viceroy was at the apex of this system; under him were various governors, civil servants, and the army. It was a formidable force, but never numbered more than 100,000 Britons in India.

Ram Raj: "Rule of Ram," the Hindu ideal of ancient India's golden age, evoked by Gandhi to mean an ideal society of harmony and justice for all religious communities, consistent with his advocacy of a secular state for independent India.

Ryot: Landless peasant or laborer.

Sadhu: A Hindu holy person, ideally with saintly qualities that Gandhi saw as consonant with political action and leadership. Also called *sannyasin.*

Sarvodaya: "Welfare of all," Gandhi's term for an ideal system of social and economic equality produced by social reforms.

Satya: Truth. A fundamental concept of Hindu philosophy. Gandhi combined the word with "*agraha,*" thus coining his key word, "*satyagraha,*" to mean literally "adherence to the truth." He believed that such adherence could produce a form of moral power.

Satyagraha: Power (or force) of truth, love, and nonviolence. The word has a broad meaning to include various forms of social and political action: individual or mass civil disobedience, as in the "salt satyagraha," or fasting for communal harmony, or campaigns for social reforms, such as for the abolition of untouchability.

Satyagrahi: One who practices the method or employs the power of *satyagraha.*

Shastras and *Smritis:* Hindu sacred texts, the subjects of Gandhi's continuing efforts at reinterpretation, especially in the contexts of orthodox views of caste and untouchability.

Swadeshi: "One's own country," meaning the principle of relying on the products of India rather than foreign goods. This often demanded boycott of British produce specifically.

Swaraj: Freedom. Gandhi interpreted the word to mean freedom in two distinct senses: the "external freedom" of political independence and "internal freedom." The latter meaning evoked the ancient Hindu (and Buddhist) idea of spiritual liberation, denoting a psychological freedom from illusion, fear, and ignorance. *Swaraj* in these two senses thus implied knowledge of self and consequent self-mastery. The idea of "freedom as self rule," conceived by the Indian nationalist movement, originally meant only political independence. Gandhi enlarged its meaning to emphasize personal as well as political liberation, necessary conditions of India's freedom, with *satyagraha* as the only way to achieve it.

Taluka: District, e.g., Bardoli, designated for purposes of land revenue collection.

Tapasya: Self-sacrifice, as in Gandhi's practice of fasting. As a form of personal renunciation, *tapasya* (or *tapas*), if practiced with purity of intent, evoked respect among Hindus. In the instance of Gandhi's Calcutta fast, he gained trust and power from his self-sacrifice.

Trusteeship: Gandhi's economic doctrine that India's privileged classes should act as trustees of their wealth, keeping for themselves only what they need, making the rest available for the public good.

Upanishads: Ancient philosophical discourses of India, regarded as main sources of Hindu metaphysics.

Varna: Social order or group, of which there were four in traditional Hindu social theory. Each *varna* had a specific social function: the *brahmin*, spiritual authority and instruction; *kshatriya*, temporal power; *vaishya*, wealth and commercial activity; and *sudra*, manual labor and service of the others. The theory of the duties and relationships of these four *varnas* was variously called *varnashrama*, *varnadharma*, or *varnashramadharma*. *Varna* is sometimes translated as caste, but Gandhi tried to distinguish them, arguing ultimately that while caste should be abolished, the system of *varna* was in theory consistent with democratic values of freedom and equality and should be preserved as a model of social harmony and cooperation.

Yajna: Sacrifice. Gandhi used this in a political sense, as *satyagraha* should be offered as a *yajna* in a spirit of sacrifice.

Yatra: Spiritual or religious pilgrimage, used by Gandhi to describe the salt march.

Zamindar: Landholder, Hindu or Muslim, paying revenue to the British.

Bibliography

Biographies

Louis Fischer, *The Life of Mahatma Gandhi* (New York: Harper, 1950) has the advantage of being written by an American journalist who visited Gandhi in India and became well-acquainted with his ideas. William L. Shirer, *Gandhi: A Memoir* (New York: Simon and Schuster, 1989), though valuable, does not pretend to be a comprehensive biography. For scholarly examinations of his life, see Judith Brown, *Gandhi: A Prisoner of Hope* (New Haven: Yale University Press, 1989), distinguished by a remarkable grasp of relevant documents, and B. R. Nanda, *Mahatma Gandhi* (Bombay: Allied Publishers, 1958), who manages to balance objective analysis with strong sympathies for Gandhi's purpose and achievements.

Theoretical Studies

Raghavan N. Iyer, *The Moral and Political Thought of Mahatma Gandhi* (New York: Oxford University Press, 1973), presents a systematic analysis of the subject that compares Gandhi's ideas throughout with western theorists. Joan Bondurant, *Conquest of Violence* (Princeton: Princeton University Press, 1988), offers original insights into the dynamics of Gandhi's use of *satyagraha* as well as an incisive examination of his emphasis on the importance of means rather than ends. Susanne and Lloyd Rudolph's *Gandhi* (Chicago: University of Chicago Press, 1983) is a penetrating analysis of the sources of Gandhi's charismatic leadership. Gene Sharp, *Gandhi as a Political Strategist* (Boston: Porter Sargent, 1979), offers a useful perspective on Gandhi's theory and practice for conflict resolution. Erik Erikson's *Gandhi's Truth* (New York: Norton, 1969) is a trenchant psychoanalytical study of Gandhi's personality as it relates to his leadership.

Anthologies

Collectors of Gandhi's writings must face the formidable task of selecting passages from his voluminous works, which now comprise one hundred volumes, entitled *The Collective Works of Mahatma Gandhi* (Delhi: Publications Division, Ministry of Information and Broadcasting, Government of India, 1958–94). Raghavan Iyer has edited a substantial segment in his three-volume *Moral and Political Writings of Mahatma Gandhi* (Oxford: Clarendon Press, 1987). This edition divides Gandhi's work into major conceptual categories, which are introduced by Iyer with his characteristically incisive analysis. Other collections, much less comprehensive and expensive than Iyer's are *The Penguin Gandhi Reader*, edited by R. Mukherjee (London and New Delhi: Penguin, 1993); *The Essential Gandhi*, edited by Louis Fischer (New York: Vintage Books, 1962), and *Gandhi: All Men Are Brothers* (New York: Continuum, 1990), edited by K. Kripalani. An awesome work on Gandhi is D. G. Tendulkar, *Mahatma* (Delhi: Government of India Publications Division, 1960) that combines large segments of his writings with exhaustive bibliography. The virtue of these eight extraordinary volumes is that they contain a close year-by-year account of Gandhi's life while integrating his own words into the historical narrative. This feat is matched only by Pyarelal and Sushila Nayar, *Mahatma Gandhi* (Ahmedabad: Navajivan, 1958–89), in the series of volumes that they have written about his life and thought. Until the recent completion of Gandhi's *Collected Works*, the Nayar opus contained comments by Gandhi unpublished elsewhere. Their books still offer incomparable perspectives from two devoted followers who were respectively Gandhi's personal secretary and personal physician.

Index